2—

MW00695533

George Iwagahi (signature)

The Japanese American Story

by Budd Fukei

DILLON PRESS, INC.
MINNEAPOLIS, MINNESOTA

Dillon Press, Inc., 500 South Third Street
Minneapolis, Minnesota 55415

Printed in the United States of America

Library of Congress Cataloging in Publication Data

Fukei, Budd.
  The Japanese-American story.
  Includes index.
    1. Japanese Americans.   2. Japanese Americans—Evacua-
tion and relocation, 1942-1945.   I. Title.
E184.J3F84   973'.04'956   75-35578
ISBN 0-87518-048-5

Contents

To my daughter, Sumi Jo, and her mother

The photographs are reproduced through the courtesy of the Brooklyn Botanic Garden, pp. 85 (bottom), 86, 87; Japanese Consulate General of Seattle, pp. 14, 19, 22, 83; Bob Miller, p. 104 (bottom); Henry H. Miyake, p. 81; George Morihiro, p. 71 (top); Northwestern National Life Insurance Company, p. 104 (top); Elmer Ogawa, p. 43 (top); Pioneer Center, Los Angeles, pp. 115, 116; **Seattle Post-Intelligencer,** pp. 33, 43 (bottom), 54; Ben Siefert, 51; "Star Trek," p. 101; War Relocation Authority (WRA) Archives, pp. 57, 58, 66; and Jack Yamaguchi, pp. 60, 61, 71 (bottom).

Foreword

Emma Lazarus's noble lines carved on the Statue of Liberty, urging the world to send its tired masses to America, were sometimes simply ironic when judged against the actual immigrant experience. Frequently, the concept of this nation as a "melting pot" was grossly erroneous.

The immigrant experience was usually painful; all the illusions about this great, golden country were shattered early. To their dismay the aliens discovered, normally in a degrading fashion, that Americans tended to judge them first and last by their appearance. This trait has been a persistent and ignominious fact in this nation's history.

For the most part, immigrants sought not to accentuate their differences. At the least, those who intended to remain here permanently generally tried to become one with the American way of life. The children, out of a sense of shame for being markedly different, often sought to out-do the native born as Americans, although as they grew older, they began to realize vaguely the value of what their parents had given them.

Though often mocked for their cultural differences, the immigrants brought much with them that has over many years enriched this society of ours. They also brought their aspirations and their craving for freedom. Always they brought hope.

These people were in many ways the best of what other nations had to offer, even if most were unlettered and unskilled. They were daring individuals, the venturesome and courageous souls. In the early days only the strongest survived the hazards of a lengthy sea voyage.

The foreigners have lasted in this land, and as they have matured, the nation has matured with them. The United States would not be the same country it is without them all — far less rich in its diverse heritage.

Those from the Orient can be readily forgiven if they found the racial slurs and the snubbings utterly intolerable. They came from societies and civilizations far older and in many respects better developed than those of the Occident. They were the products of cultures as profound and as enduring as any the world has seen.

All too many times in the West they were treated as heathens capable only of coolie labor. They were looked on as people from a world apart. To their honor, they persevered and established themselves. Therefore, it is eminently suitable that a book on the Japanese place in American society be written. Budd Fukei has unusual qualifications for the task. He is not so old as to be unaware of the viewpoints of the young, nor is he so young as not to be firmly acquainted with the traditions and inheritance of the old.

Americans have not chronicled the immigrant experience as thoroughly as we might have. This book is worth reading, not only as a record of one Japanese experience, but also because Mr. Fukei, an excellent journalist, has written it with warm understanding and colorful sympathy. He has told the story honestly, but with a gentle forbearance, demonstrating in print the tolerance we preach but infrequently practice.

One assumes the book will be of principal interest to the Japanese. It should not be so. We all should be aware of what was added to this nation when these very vital and energetic people came to our shores. Out of this might come a clearer understanding of what we are as Americans and the meaning that resides in our history.

Those of us who are the children of immigrants, especially of those whose language was not English, should gain a perspective on our own lives that is not easily obtained. The disdain with which we saw our parents rebuffed, the hurts we watched them suffer and even endured ourselves, are too deep and too personal to make that perspective easily realizable.

Over the years we have largely overcome such an invalid sense of inferiority. We have come to be respected, whatever our race, creed, or national origin. It should be repeated that the early immigrants were truly the brave and the bold.

Rolf Stromberg, formerly Arts and Drama
Editor – Seattle Post Intelligencer

Preface

My daughter could not have been more than five or six years old when she came home one afternoon and wondered aloud why she was "different." Some of her playmates had remarked about her racial background. I remember well the troubled expression on her face as I explained to her that she was an American just like her friends. Except, I added, she was of Japanese ancestry on my side of the family and Scotch-Irish, French, and German on her mother's side. Then I explained that hers was a beautiful blend of rich cultures handed down from both her mother's and father's parents. The explanation satisfied the concerned child. Smiling, she hurried back to her friends. That was probably the first time my daughter had ever been truly conscious of her Japanese ancestry. It is sufficient reason for me to hope this book will help her and others who have Japanese parents realize that theirs is a proud, much-respected heritage.

Despite my own involvement, I have attempted to be objective in my dual role of observer and chronicler. If I appear to be in closer touch with Seattle than with any other city, it is because I know Seattle best. I was born, reared, and educated there. Since the early 1900s, most Seattle Japanese have lived in an area which, in contemporary jargon, would be called a ghetto. Here, the Japanese immigrants (the *Issei*) eked out a livelihood, saved money, and sent their children to school. Their children (the *Nisei*) studied hard. Many earned scholastic honors in high schools and colleges and went on to succeed in their chosen professions. Important factors in overcoming adverse social conditions were the interest and moral support given by their families and the Issei community in general. It is greatly to the credit of the Japanese immigrants that they were eager to preserve the traditions and culture they brought to this country. This amalgamation of old culture and new culture came easily for them because they had a deep feeling for history as well as an awareness of what the future could bring.

The Japanese came to this country with the basic belief in the things that America stood for — equality, opportunity, and freedom. They were able to maintain this faith despite the prejudice and even hatred that culminated in the internment of Japanese Americans during World War II. I subscribe to this faith myself, and hopefully I have done my part — without bias — to reinforce the bridge between these two cultures.

I purposely selected a wide range of topics in this book in order to provide the reader with a better understanding of the Japanese culture and therefore a better understanding of the Japanese residing in the United States.

The main characters in this book are the Issei, the first Japanese immigrants, and their children, the Nisei. In a supporting role are the non-Japanese whose presence helped create *The Japanese American Story*. Of the latter, the kind inspired while the unkind helped to toughen and strengthen the Japanese community. Like other immigrants, the Japanese formed societies of their own. They clustered together to protect themselves and to maintain a united spirit.

Today the Japanese are spreading out in the community. They no longer live in their cramped business quarters as many did before World War II. They are fast becoming suburban homeowners. Assimilation and intermarriages are becoming commonplace. The *Sansei* (third-generation Japanese Americans) and the *Yonsei* (fourth-generation Japanese Americans) are beginning to assert themselves socially.

If the reader should acquire even a particle of knowledge

about the Japanese, credit must be shared with those who generously assisted me and contributed their thoughts. The shortcomings are mine alone. It is with gratitude I acknowledge the assistance received from Bob Okazaki, a former Seattleite now residing in Los Angeles; Ed Groshell, formerly of the military publication *Stars & Stripes,* Tokyo; Harry Honda, editor, *Pacific Citizen,* Los Angeles; Dr. Minoru Masuda and Dr. Frank S. Miyamoto, both of the University of Washington; Takami Hibiya, editor, *The North American Post,* Seattle; Yas Abiko, editor, *Nichibei Times,* and Howard Imazeki, editor, *Hokubei Mainichi,* both of San Francisco; Yutaka Hirano, associate editor, *Nisei Veterans Newsletter* of Seattle; and friends such as Mr. and Mrs. George Tokuda, Yukio Kuniyuki, Victor Abe, Mrs. Kats Kunitsugu and Kunio Otani.

Other sources helpful to my work include the Seattle chapter of the Japanese American Citizens League; the Learning Center of Fort Steilacoom Community College of Tacoma, Washington; Puyallup Valley Citizens League of Washington; the Seattle Public Library; and the cooperative libraries and the librarians of the University of Washington, the University of California, Berkeley, the University of California at Los Angeles (UCLA), and the Japanese American Research Project.

I should also like to mention Seattle public school teachers Elizabeth Rowell, Amelia Telban, Grace Reiner, and Ira T. Miller, as well as the late Professor Howard Brier of the School of Journalism of the University of Washington, for their encouragement during my earliest efforts to write.

Finally, my sincerest thanks to Uva Dillon, the publisher, for giving me the opportunity to write this book.

Budd Fukei

1.
The Japanese in Japan: Their Origin

No one knows for sure where the first Japanese came from. Japan's early records mix mythical tradition with legendary history and actual historical events. But though the records are a jumble of truth and fiction, the underlying message is clear: the Japanese were a special people with a special place in history.

According to legend, the universe was a chaotic mass in the beginning. From out of the early chaos, the lightest mass moved steadily upward to form the High Plain of Heaven, in which dwelled the invisible Kami, who were superior beings. After several generations of Kami, there appeared Izanagi, the Great Celestial Being, and his mate, Izanami.

Chosen to subdue the chaos on earth, these two descended on the Bridge of Heaven. As he set foot on earth, Izanagi dipped his jeweled spear into its deep blue waters. As he withdrew his weapon from the water, the brine which clung to the tip of his dazzling spear dropped back into the sea to become Orogoro, the first of the Japanese islands.

On this island, Izanagi and Izanami begot the other Japanese islands. Izanami also gave birth to many Kami, including the Kami of fire. She died from the burns suffered during this birth and descended into the underworld.

In the hope of recovering his mate, Izanagi traveled to the lower world and entered the land of the night. Because Izanami had eaten within this land, she was not allowed to return. As Izanami sought permission to leave, Izanagi glanced upon her

The seal of Amaterasu, the goddess of the sun, was used in feudal Japan.

face and saw it was in a state of decay. Horrified, he fled the underworld.

Returning to the upper world, Izanagi stopped to bathe. As he disrobed, twelve Kami were created from his various articles of clothing, among them the Kami of the moon, the Kami of the wind, and Amaterasu, the Kami of the sun, who came to be known as the ''goddess of the sun.''

With Amaterasu, we begin to cross the line from myth to legendary history. Amaterasu's great-great-great grandson was Jimmu Tenno, the Heavenly Emperor who founded the first Japanese empire in the year 660 B.C. Thus the legend of Amaterasu opens the sliding door to Japan's past, with Jimmu Tenno as Japan's first quasi-historical figure.

Today, Amaterasu is worshipped at a sacred shrine, Ise, in central Japan, but only the emperor is allowed inside the shrine. Until the end of World War II, every emperor visited the shrine to pay homage to the Sun Goddess and to report to her all events of national importance. The emperor himself was believed to rule by divine right, and he could do no wrong. Prince Hirobumi Ito, who was largely responsible for the Japanese Constitution of 1889, wrote, "The emperor is heaven-descended, divine and sacred; he is pre-eminent above his subjects. He must be reverenced and is inviolable . . . ."[1] Until January 1, 1946, when Emperor Hirohito renounced this belief, whenever the emperor made a public appearance, all windows and doors were closed, and no one dared gaze at the emperor's face.

Writings of the Shinto religion list an unbroken line of monarchs who have reigned over Japan since 660 B.C. However, historians dismiss the early emperors, before A.D. 300, as mythical figures. Those after A.D. 300 are regarded as historical. The Japanese entombed many of their emperors in stone chambers with plastered walls. Strange as it may seem, the question of opening the tombs to discover more about the early Japanese people never arose prior to World War II. Such a move would have shown great disrespect for the throne.

In the spring of 1972, the Japanese government permitted scholars to open a tomb near Nara in central Japan where they found what was reported to be one of the greatest art discoveries of the century. Sixteen brilliantly colored figures of men and women in ancient Asian dress were painted on the plaster walls of the tomb. On the ceiling was a huge painting of a bear. These paintings, historians say, came from the Asuka period of Japanese art (A.D. 552-646), which just preceded the time of the formation of Japan's first central government.

Archaeological evidence indicates that most early Japanese came to the Japanese islands from Korea. These migrations probably occurred sometime in the first century A.D. Other Japanese may have come from northeastern and southeastern Asia and southern China. Since then, of course, the Japanese have mixed with people of central Asia, the Middle East, and Europe. Now there is no "typical" Japanese, for the people exhibit different combinations of genetic types.

Himeji Castle, built in 1609, represents the splendor of feudal Japan.

Most experts agree that the Ainu, a people of Caucasoid stock, were the first to settle on the Japanese islands. But the Ainus suffered a fate similar to that of the Indians in America. The Ainus were overwhelmed by immigrants from the Asiatic mainland and Southeast Asia.

According to one historian, the early Japanese settlers from Korea organized into clans and eventually formed the Yamato court, which loosely controlled central and western Japan. This was the first Japanese government. In a way, the Koreans are the direct ancestors of the present imperial family.[2]

The artifacts of the Korean invaders reveal an earlier contact with Chinese civilization. Therefore, much of the Japanese culture was derived from the Chinese, though indirectly, through the Koreans. Later, the Japanese were influenced directly by their contact with Chinese traders. During the period from the sixth century through the ninth century, Japan made a tremendous effort to absorb Chinese culture. The introduction of Buddhism and its surrounding arts occurred during this time. The Yamato court attempted, during the early seventh century, to become a miniature Chinese centralized state, and Japanese architecture of this period shows great similarity to the Chinese model.

Japan's obvious desire to learn from China was replaced in the ninth century by a new cultural independence. During the next period of about 350 years, called the classical age, the earlier Japanese borrowings became distinctly Japanese. Japanese writing, though still containing Chinese characters, achieved a distinctive form. The emperor served merely as a weak figurehead in the government at this time. Power was situated in families or clans.

The period preceding the 1600s brought increasing political chaos, and the desire for political stability outweighed other forces. In the 1630s, the Tokugawa family broke off Japan's contacts with the outside world in order to strengthen their political control and to fortify the political system itself. The Tokugawas restored political tranquility until the middle of the nineteenth century, but in doing so they suppressed much creativity and brought about a halt in cultural development. Japan now fell far behind China and Europe.

In looking back at the early history of Japan, second-generation Americans of Japanese ancestry (the *Nisei*) have been willing to accept the historical events but not the mythical tradition of Japan. Their immigrant parents (the *Issei*) may speak in glowing terms of the Sun Goddess, Amaterasu, and the Nisei learn about the myth in their studies at Japanese language schools, but just as some Christians question whether God created Adam and Eve, many of the Nisei have not been able to accept the Amaterasu legend on faith. The still more western-ized *Sansei* (third-generation Japanese Americans) are skeptical about the mythological origin of Japan, but the myth nevertheless fascinates them.

It is these American offspring of Japanese immigrants — and the mixture of East and West they represent — that are the subject of this book.

An Issei grandmother with her Sansei granddaughter, at a Japanese festival in Seattle, Washington.

2.
The Japanese
Discover America

In spite of Japan's isolation from the rest of the world, a slowly growing industrial class had emerged by the early nineteenth century. The economy was still based largely on agriculture, but the new industries would benefit greatly from trade with other countries. It is not difficult to see why Commodore Perry's arrival in the 1850s was followed by such turmoil and rapid change.

Although Perry's arrival in Japanese ports was preceded by Russian and English overtures to Japan, it was the American, with a formidable fleet of warships, who successfully persuaded Japan to open her doors. The American commodore showered top Japanese officials with many American products — champagne and whiskey, rifles and revolvers, clocks and sewing machines, a miniature locomotive, a telegraph outfit, perfume, and books. The dramatic introduction of foreign civilization produced a great disruption in Japan, out of which arose a new political state — the Meiji government — and a change from an agricultural economy to industrialism.

Those most hurt by the shift were, naturally, the farmers and rural workers, and they were among the first to emigrate to America. The Japanese move to industrialism happened at a time when America badly needed unskilled agricultural help. In the 1860s, Japan allowed a number of workers to emigrate to Hawaii and California in order to work on the farms. Until well into the twentieth century Japan placed restrictions on the number of Japanese leaving Japan, and in the early years was extremely watchful of the emigrants' welfare in America.

The greatest influx of Japanese immigrants to the United States was between 1890 and 1907, after which immigration was severely limited by the Gentleman's Agreement, which stopped the flow of laborers to the Pacific coast. The American government required that the Japanese confine the issuing of passports to former U.S. residents, relatives of residents, and settled agriculturalists.

The Gentleman's Agreement was not the first or only legal action demonstrating prejudice against Japanese Americans, though before World War II, the United States government tried to avoid seriously offending the Japanese government. In California, the fear of Oriental predominance in agriculture resulted in a buildup of prejudice in that state. In 1906, San Francisco enacted a ruling which forced Japanese children to attend special Oriental schools. In 1913, a law was passed in California denying aliens the right to own land. The Japanese, as Asiatics, were not eligible for naturalization, and this law directly affected their security in the United States. Finally, in 1924, a law was passed which duplicated an earlier Chinese Exclusion Act, and excluded Japanese solely on the basis of race. The law was a serious insult to the Japanese government, and the strained relations were eased only slowly and indirectly by individual gestures of goodwill between Japanese and Americans.

Although most Japanese immigrants were agriculturalists, other Japanese did settle in America. Discovering the country meant entirely different things to these different people. Some left their homeland to dodge military duty. Others wanted to tear themselves away from a life dictated by the harsh rules of Japanese social order. The sons of samurai were attracted to the educational opportunities. Many came because of the rumors of vast wealth in America. Each one came with hopes of bettering his station in life.

The first Japanese on record to venture onto United States soil

Mount Fuji or Fujiyama, Japan's highest peak, a symbol of the homeland to many Issei.

was Manjiro Nakahama. His discovery of America was dictated by fate rather than design. He was a shipwrecked sailor who was rescued with four others by an American whaler from a tiny uninhabited island in the Pacific. Manjiro was fourteen, and the year was 1841. William H. Whitfield, the captain of the ship, took a liking to the youngster and brought him back to his home in Massachusetts, where Manjiro received a formal education.

Some years later, Manjiro returned to Japan. He found that entering Japan was not all that easy, even for a Japanese. When he reentered his country, he was questioned by Japanese officials, and held for a year and a half before he was allowed to return to his family.

The family reunion for Manjiro lasted only three days, for he was immediately asked to teach science and English at a Japanese school. There, he often described America and its people. His firsthand information came as quite a revelation to the Japanese, who had been living for so long in isolation.

In 1860, Manjiro served as the official interpreter and navigation instructor in a goodwill mission sent by Japan to the United States. Japan's first ambassador to the United States, Norimasa Muragaki, was second in command of the Japanese mission. He recorded many events of this trip to America. The excerpts from his diary show his surprise at the American style of living.[3]

Muragaki described the train ride across the Isthmus of Panama:

> With a thundering noise, the train began to move forward.... The noise it made became as deafening as an endless series of thunderclaps and several feet away from the carriage all things, trees and plants, seemed to run in horizontal stripes. The feeling was exactly the same as galloping on horseback.

He recalled the trip up the Potomac River to the nation's capital:

> Some ten miles from the City of Washington we saw on the left bank of the river a large building shaded by trees which we were told was the house where

George Washington had lived. Farther up the river there stood on the right bank a monument looking like a fortress. This, we learned, was Washington's tomb. In passing by his tomb, every ship halts awhile and has its band play music, while all the passengers and crew take their hats off in homage to the Father of the Nation—this custom, well-grounded as it is, is worthy of note as occurring in the nation free of all manner of formality.

The Japanese were presented to President James Buchanan.

We felt slightly put out of countenance when we discovered that the Americans attached little importance to class distinction and dispensed with all manners of decorum....It seemed to us a most curious custom to permit the presence of ladies on such a ceremonious occasion as today....

After dinner, we were ushered into another large room, the floor of which was covered with smooth boards. In one corner, music was played on instruments which looked like fiddles. Officers in uniform with epaulets and swords and ladies dressed in *robes decolletés* of light white material and wide skirts began, couple by couple, moving around the room, walking on tiptoe to the tune of the music.

I was quite amused to watch the way in which the ladies' voluminous skirts spread to an enormous proportion, as their wearers took quick turns. Upon inquiring, we were told that this was what is called a "waltz" and that even officials of high rank and elderly ladies, as well as young people, were very fond of this pastime....This, we were told, would continue all night. We stood there gaping at this amazing sight such as we had never seen or dreamed of.

The Japanese had five days in New York before sailing to Southampton, England, so Manjiro used the time to visit Captain Whitfield. "Manjiro," Kaneko writes, "gave Captain Whitfield and his family and all his former friends many gifts which he had brought from Japan—lacquer boxes, silk cloth, kimonos, Japanese color prints."[4]

Today, a statue of Manjiro stands near his native village in Japan. The statue was built in commemoration of the Meiji centennial and was unveiled in 1968.

Perhaps the most important of these first Japanese immigrants was Hikozo Hamada. Like Manjiro, Hikozo was rescued on the high seas. The year was 1850 and Hikozo, then thirteen years old, was sailing with his father on a trading voyage when their vessel was shipwrecked in a storm. The castaways drifted for fifty days until sighted and rescued by an American ship.

The ship's captain transported Hikozo and sixteen of his shipmates to San Francisco, where Hikozo and two other friends decided to become Americans and Californians. Subsequently, Hikozo took the name Joseph Heco. For a time, Heco and his friends attempted to make their fortune by mining gold, but with no success. Then they began working as stewards aboard American ships. But Heco, who was intelligent and adventurous, soon was offered a chance to go to school. He was

Stone lanterns (foreground) against the Great Torii near the Inland Sea, the gateway to the Itsukushima Shrine in Japan.

taken to a Catholic school in Baltimore, where he eventually became a naturalized American citizen. (It was later in the century that laws were passed 'denying Asians the right of naturalization.) Shortly after he became an American citizen, Heco was offered an appointment to West Point by President Franklin Pierce. Heco declined the offer, saying he preferred the Catholic university.

In 1858, Heco was named captain's clerk (and interpreter) with a surveying expedition in the Pacific. Although seasickness forced him to leave the ship when it docked in Hawaii, he managed to travel to Japan where he went into business as a commission merchant. In 1861, he returned to San Francisco and then continued to Washington, where, in 1862, he was appointed interpreter for the American Consulate in Kanagawa (now Yokohama). Heco thus became the first American of Japanese ancestry to serve the United States government.

For the typical Japanese American immigrant, however, life has been far more difficult, requiring much hard work and perseverance, as the story of Suekichi F. shows. Suekichi F. came to the United States in the early nineteen hundreds to escape the burden of the rice fields, where he toiled for his room and board at his aunt's farm in Shiga prefecture, Japan. He had lost both parents when he was fifteen years old. A small fellow, he was a scant one hundred pounds and not much more than five feet tall—wholly unfit for this labor which, after eleven years, had nearly worn him out. Suekichi got to thinking more and more about the foreign land which he had heard was covered with gold.

One day he received a letter. A friend had written to him from America, urging him to journey to that country. Suekichi decided to call on his aunt, for in order to get to America, he would need money.

"Please," he pleaded as he gazed at his knotty hands which had worked miles and miles of rice paddies. "There's a fortune for anyone who is willing to work."

His aunt knew the young man had worked hard all his life. He was bright, honest, cheerful. Why not? She agreed to lend him some money.

The other young men from the farm cast envious glances at Suekichi as he boarded the train for Yokohama. *"Shikkari hataraki nasai!"* (Work hard!) *"Karada o daijini shinasai!"* (Take care of yourself!)

At Yokohama, Suekichi took a steamship that was headed for the United States by way of Vancouver. The ships took twenty days or more to cross the Pacific. Sometimes the ocean was calm and tranquil, but the immigrants also remembered days and nights when the ships pitched and rolled because of the ocean's awesome strength.

After a day's pause in Canada, Suekichi and the others transferred to a slow steamship bound for the United States. On the afternoon of the day they boarded, the cry of "A-me-li-ka! A-me-li-ka!" echoed throughout the ship. The passengers strained their eyes, focusing them on the narrow body of water, which they later learned was Puget Sound, and on the jagged mountains on either side of it. As the steamship docked at Seattle, Suekichi was suddenly seized by qualms about his coming. Everywhere Suekichi turned there were big, husky longshoremen. Must he compete with them for work?

Suekichi searched and searched through a sea of faces for the man who was to meet him and his fellow immigrants. Finally he saw a well-dressed Japanese man waiting nearby. The man took Suekichi and the others in the group to a hotel. Soon thereafter, Suekichi went to the Japanese employment agency to inquire about jobs.

Suekichi worked both in the sawmills and on the railroads. But sawmill and railroad hours sapped his strength and spirit. At the end of every bone-weary day, the men cooked their meals over an open fire outside their bunkhouses—rain, shine, or snow. After dinner, many stayed up and talked or read letters from home. Some gambled to pass the time away, and others went directly to bed from sheer exhaustion.

Always after a rainy day, the workers placed their drenched shoes to dry in the warmest spot in the bunkhouse. The next day, the men limped to work, for the dried shoes had taken different shapes, and their feet hurt. The men had no spare pair of shoes. It was difficult, but Suekichi plugged along, leading a spartan life, scrimping and saving.

Often, when the night air was clear and the moon shone brightly, Suekichi sat on a tree stump outside the bunkhouse. Sadness welled up in his heart as he contemplated his future in the wilderness. He knew he had to make good, for the thought always in the back of his mind was of the money he had borrowed from his aunt.

Days turned to weeks and weeks to months. Finally, Suekichi had had enough of sawmill and railroad work. It was back to the city and back to the Japanese employment agency.

Suekichi was told that a Mr. Richardson wanted a maintenance man for his apartment in the Capitol Hill district, then one of Seattle's posh areas.

"What's your name?" Mr. Richardson asked.

"Suekichi," the young man answered brightly.

"Su-ye...what?"

"Suekichi."

"Oh! Let's make it Sam."

And "Sam" he was at the Richardsons' for the next five years, where he was looked after as if he were their own son, and was treated with kindness by the tenants.

Working at the Richardsons', Suekichi accumulated more than enough money for the return trip home and to pay his debt to his aunt in Japan. He married a girl from the village where he had spent his boyhood, and they took the long voyage back across the Pacific to start life anew in America.

The couple settled in Seattle, and Suekichi tried his hand at several businesses: a fruit stand, a hand laundry, and even a dye works. He bought and later sold an apartment house. He managed a hotel and then worked for the Japanese Language School. His wife helped him as much as she could, and they worked very hard to provide for their son and daughter.

At the beginning of World War II, Suekichi's son was inducted into the United States Army; later, he was rejected as physically unfit and was sent home. With his family's permission, Suekichi's son left for the Midwest in March of 1942 to find a job. A month later, Suekichi, his wife, and his daughter were among the thousands led into concentration camps. First, they were "guests of the nation" at the Puyallup (Washington) Fairgrounds, which served as an assembly center, and several months later they were moved to Minidoka, Idaho.

In 1945, after nearly three years in the evacuation center, Suekichi and his wife were offered free transportation back to Seattle, and room and board for the rest of their lives. After much thought about why they were chosen to receive this gift and much persuasion from their friends, the Suekichis accepted the offer. Later, their friends received similar gifts from the government.

After a few years of "Which restaurant shall we go to today?" and "What shall we eat?" the two tired of government handouts. The idea of welfare disturbed them. At sixty-six, Suekichi was too old to start looking for work, but his wife was still fairly young and strong. They returned the meal tickets and the room checks to a government agency. Mrs. Suekichi began to do housework for other families, and the proud couple never went back to the agency.

In 1952, the Congress of the United States passed the Walter-McCarran Immigration and Naturalization Act, which did away with race as a qualification for naturalization and gave Japanese aliens the long overdue right to become American citizens. Japanese American Citizens League (JACL) chapters throughout the nation assisted the aliens by conducting naturalization classes. One of the chapters was in Seattle, and one of those enrolled in class was Suekichi.

On November 16, 1953, at seventy-four years of age, Suekichi became an American citizen. Although he was too old to take advantage of all the benefits of citizenship, Suekichi was

This "I am an American Day" banquet was sponsored by the Japanese community to honor Issei who joined the ranks of naturalized American citizens.

happy to be a genuine American. Scores of other Japanese never bothered to apply for citizenship because they felt it was too late in life, but Suekichi wanted to be a real part of America.

Suekichi was born May 18, 1879, a Japanese citizen. He died May 24, 1964, an American citizen. He was but one among thousands of hard-working Japanese who chose America as their country.

3.
Pearl Harbor and Persecution

In the years just before World War II, as tensions were building up between the United States and Japan, many Japanese Americans began to wonder what would happen to them if war did break out between the two countries. In December 1940, a letter asking this very question was written by a young Nisei to Boake Carter, a prominent radio commentator. Carter replied in part as follows:

> I do not think war between Japan and the United States is in view at the present moment. If it did occur, it would be primarily a naval war. If fought in the Pacific, it would be to a strong disadvantage to the U.S. Fleet on the axiom that a fleet operating more than 2,000 miles from its base loses 40 percent of its fighting efficiency. If war occurred between the two nations, American born Japanese would suffer primarily because of the unthinking hysteria of an emotional public.[5]

A year later, Pearl Harbor. And four months after that, the evacuation. Pearl Harbor was to crush the hopes of the Japanese Americans for the duration of the war. That day marked the beginning of what became their greatest ordeal. It was a cycle which took them to American concentration camps; to the cities of the Rocky Mountains, the Midwest, and the East Coast; to the battlefields in Europe and the Far East; and finally, after nearly four years, back home again.

Preceding World War II there was a buildup of prejudice on the West Coast. The Japanese were resented and distrusted for several reasons; the most important was their unusual success in agriculture. The skill of Japanese workers enabled them to move quickly from their positions as agricultural help to become independent tenant farmers. The more efficient methods used by the Japanese brought financial loss to other independent farmers and a fear of Japanese predominance in agriculture in areas of the West Coast. Before the alien land laws were enacted, there was a steady increase in the number of Japanese farmers working independently in California.

Another reason Japanese were distrusted was their tendency to cluster together into "Little Tokyos." However, they did this for reasons of survival. Discrimination by Caucasians denied suitable employment to the better-educated Japanese Americans, and all Japanese Americans had difficulty in obtaining necessary services. They gathered together to achieve some self-sufficiency. Looking back at the prejudice and discrimination in the years before World War II, it is not surprising that citizens' groups seeking economic gain and politicians seeking favor with the voters insisted on internment, if not deportation. And it is not surprising that the attack on Pearl Harbor caused much anxiety among Japanese Americans about their futures in America.

A Japanese remembered:"'My first reaction to the attack was utter disbelief that such a thing could happen. Then I had a real sinking feeling of wondering what would be the consequences as far as our personal lives were concerned.''

One Japanese man was fishing off the Pacific coast and did not know anything about the attack until he drove into a service station on his way home. A passerby, noticing him sitting at the steering wheel of his car, growled, "I'll be coming back after you tonight—with my gun.''

A man who had been a sophomore in high school when the war broke out recalled that he dreaded going to school on Monday, December 8, to face his friends and classmates. However, the principal of the school assembled the students to hear President Roosevelt's war message to Congress via radio, and after this, the principal asked for fair treatment of the ten Nisei attending the school. He warned the students not to blame the war on the Nisei simply because they happened to be of the same ancestry as the enemy in Japan who attacked Pearl Harbor. A teacher of German descent told of hard times experienced by her parents during World War I, and she, too, pleaded that the Japanese Americans at the school be treated fairly.

Another Japanese American remembers an entirely different experience: "I was a junior....I do remember the initial disbelief followed by a feeling of embarrassment, and then resentment when my math instructor called me to the front of the class on Monday to ask me how I felt about the Pearl Harbor incident."

Following the attack on Pearl Harbor, martial law was declared in Hawaii. Individual Japanese Americans who aroused any kind of suspicion were apprehended, and Nisei serving in the National Guard were deactivated. However, only about one thousand were evacuated to the mainland. One might well ask why the Japanese Americans in Hawaii were not immediately interned since this is where the Japanese attack took place. The reason for this is that they were almost 40 percent of the population and a large segment of the labor force. True, there were pressures by certain military officials to move them, but there were also counterpressures in Hawaii by officials who knew the importance of the Japanese American labor force and who were more trusting of their loyalty.

Japanese American communities on the West Coast were suddenly separated from the rest of the society. The inhabitants now found themselves seen not as American residents or citizens, but as enemies of the United States—just because they were of Japanese ancestry. Many non-Oriental Americans declared that Japanese Americans were unwilling or unable to assimilate and did not belong. Japanese Americans often heard the phrase "God damn Japs!" Some were even spat on or physically injured. And, in the name of patriotism, members of other minorities turned their backs on the Japanese. Orientals displayed "China" or "Philippine" buttons to advise non-Orientals that they were not Japanese. Huge signs were posted declaring, "This is a Chinese-American restaurant." Businesses owned by the Japanese were investigated, and some were vandalized by "patriotic" citizens.

Bowing to a protest petition from a delegation of mothers from a district in West Seattle, twenty-three Japanese women employed as clerks in Seattle's elementary schools all resigned. They expressed the following sentiments in a letter to the School Board:

> We do not take this action in any spirit of defeat, but believe we can by our resignations demonstrate beyond dispute that we have the best interests of the school system at heart. We take this step to prove our loyalty to the schools and the United States by not becoming a contributing factor to dissension and disunity when national unity in spirit and deed is vitally necessary to the defense of and complete victory for America.[6]

Meanwhile, one thousand University of Washington students signed a petition urging reinstatement of the clerks and deploring the mothers' action as "undemocratic, intolerant, disrespectful of the rights of American citizens, and detrimental to the best interests of the community."

A congressional committee, headed by Representative John Tolan of California, visited Seattle during the latter part of February 1942, in order to hold a hearing on "problems of evacuation of enemy aliens and others from prohibited military zones."[7] During the hearing, people argued that American-born Japanese had within their ranks potential saboteurs, that they were more alien than those of German and Italian descent, and that Seattle shouldn't "depend upon the enemy" to feed it.[8] Opponents of evacuation pointed out that some persons sponsoring the move had selfish interests in the problem and that wholesale evacuation was not necessary. They suggested that it be done only as a last resort.[9]

On February 19, 1942, President Franklin D. Roosevelt signed an executive order to relocate all West Coast Japanese. The edict was signed before the Tolan Committee had returned to Washington, D.C., to report its findings on the Japanese.

Beginning in March 1942, West Coast Japanese were moved to assembly centers, most of which were located in California. From the assembly centers, the Japanese were moved to relocation centers, which were scattered primarily in the Midwest and California. During the detention, legislation was passed which further restricted the Japanese following their release. What most hurt the Japanese was a tightening of alien land laws. During and after evacuation, land held by the Japanese was confiscated. The alien land laws were not declared unconstitutional until several years after the return of the Japanese to their homes.

People swept gleefully down on Japanese American homes and businesses to dicker for family possessions, furniture, and retail goods. Families were forced to part with their material belongings which they had accumulated over the years. Particularly hard hit were those who were approaching retirement years, for the Japanese Americans had no choice but to sell at ridiculously low prices. As if to tighten the economic noose, the government froze the assets of those who had accounts in Japanese branch banks in the United States. (Thirty years later—October 3, 1972—President Nixon signed a law which enabled Japanese who were interned or paroled during World War II to file claims with the Office of Alien Property of the Department of Justice for payment of their prewar yen certificates of deposit in the Yokohama Specie Bank.)

A number of people lost their leases on hotels, restaurants, grocery stores, variety shops, and clothing stores. In fact, those who didn't lose their business establishments were the exception, not the rule.

Japanese Americans living outside the evacuation area were

A soldier nails up placards explaining Civilian Exclusion Order No. 1, the beginning of the evacuation and relocation of West Coast Japanese.

also "punished" for the attack on Pearl Harbor. Kunio Ishii and his wife in Ely, Nevada, remember the day their eldest daughter, then only seven years old, came home from school one day with her clothes torn, crying, "They threw rocks at me." Ann Muranaka, a friend of the Ishiis, lived in the same town. Her husband was one of the "leaders" who were whisked to an internment camp in Missoula, Montana. Muranaka's money was frozen by the government, so his wife had an extremely difficult time making ends meet. She managed somehow, though, until her husband was released. The two relocated to Chicago, and later they went back to Japan. Six years later, Muranaka died. A grieving Mrs. Muranaka returned to the United States with her husband's ashes. Heartbroken over the loss of her husband and the unhappy war years, she died shortly afterwards. She could have avoided all the unpleasantness, but she chose to stand by her husband. Mrs. Muranaka was Caucasian.

As a whole, the Japanese Americans cooperated with the government at every turn. Their Eastern stoicism combined with Western ingenuity helped sustain them. The Issei frequently turned to the Nisei for advice because the Nisei had a better grasp of the English language and a better understanding of what the government expected of them.

They also had developed a strong organization, the Japanese American Citizens League (JACL), which bore the brunt of responsibility during this shaky period. As early as 1940, the leaders of the JACL pledged that in case of conflict between Japan and the United States, "we are Americans first." This was true of most other Japanese Americans, too. Even before their loyalty was questioned, the Japanese Americans made statements vowing allegiance to the United States, bought defense bonds, offered to donate blood, and willingly served in the armed forces. Even after evacuation, most of them remained patriotic Americans.

It may well appear surprising to the reader that the Japanese Americans accepted internment and lived through this hostile period so quietly. However, traditional Japanese teachings emphasize values—obedience, allegiance to authority, and self-control—which, in this situation, would not allow an emotional protest. True, the Japanese in the United States valued individual freedom and those who were citizens were aware of their rights. But they were also aware of the threat of economic, social, and political reprisals hovering over their lives during the early months of World War II. Thus, when the first big evacuation was started, the Japanese Americans voiced little protest, mainly because they felt their chances for fair treatment were zero in a climate of war hysteria.

4.
Why the Japanese Americans Cooperated

In 1941, Mike Masaru Masaoka was an instructor in the speech department at the University of Utah. During that year, he was approached by the JACL to become its first full-time, paid staff member. After much deliberation with friends, he resigned his job at the university and accepted the JACL offer. Right away, Masaoka sensed the seriousness of the problems faced by Japanese Americans in case of war between Japan and America.

Shortly after Japan's attack on Pearl Harbor, talk of evacuation and detention surfaced in the United States. Masaoka and other JACL leaders knew then that the Japanese Americans were in deep trouble for no other reason than the fact that they were born Japanese. When the decision was finally made to evacuate and confine Japanese Americans, Masaoka was among those who saw the futility of resistance. He knew that the nation's wartime mood made it in the best interests of the Japanese to go along with the evacuation and eventually detention. Masaoka and the JACL worked hard to help the government carry out an orderly mass movement while keeping faith in American justice and fair play. Masaoka's recollections of that period are given in the remainder of this chapter.

THE EVACUATION DECISION

More than thirty years after the fact, it is difficult to remember all of the circumstances that caused some of us, then leaders of the Japanese American Citizens League, to decide that we of Japanese ancestry should cooperate with the government in our own evacuation and detention in the spring of 1942. But there are many aspects that contributed to the temper of those times that I can still recall as having forced me, among others, to conclude that cooperation at that time was the best, and only, course of action for our people to follow.

In this connection, it should be kept in mind that we young Nisei in the JACL leadership, then averaging about thirty years of age, had to make the fateful decision that would affect the lives and the fortunes of more than 110,000 men, women, and children, of all ages and in all conditions of health, not only for the immediate future but for years and possibly generations to come.

If we could have acted as individuals and had not been responsible for the destiny of a whole minority group in its most critical period, some of us might—and probably would have —reacted differently. But we did assume the responsibility for the total Japanese population on the Pacific Coast, and often suffered, as a result, severe criticism and even bodily injury. It would have been easier on us as individuals to have avoided that awesome responsibility, but we could not think and act as individuals, accountable only to ourselves and our own self-interest. We were answerable to, and for, the Japanese on the West Coast, so we had to think and act on behalf of all of the people concerned.

We in the JACL did not want to assume the leadership of those of Japanese ancestry since we all had personal and family problems of our own to take care of, but we had no choice if there was to be any leadership at that critical time. Practically every Japanese American organization, except the Christian churches, became defunct after December 7, 1941, and almost every Issei leader was arrested for one reason or another by the FBI and interned soon after the attack on Pearl Harbor. If the JACL had not stepped in to provide the leadership, there would have been panic and chaos in the various Japanese American communities in the western states.

Some Japanese language newspapers were shut down immediately following the Japanese attack, so the JACL had to provide news and information concerning the intentions and programs of the government—national, state, and local. Personal bank accounts were frozen, so the JACL had to persuade Washington to allow the withdrawal of small amounts in order to purchase the bare necessities of life. Many Japanese American businesses were closed down, and many Japanese Americans were summarily fired from their jobs. Other workers would not plant or harvest crops on farms operated by Japanese Americans. In some cases the families of those who were interned had to be taken care of. So many people were out of work that the JACL had to go into the welfare business. Some stores would not sell goods, including medical supplies, to Japanese Americans, so that special arrangements had to be made for necessary purchases. Plans had to be readied to protect as much as possible the lives and property of Japanese Americans from vandalism, arson, and even mob violence.

For understandable reasons, most public officials were reluctant to cooperate with the JACL even in such simple matters as welfare and home protection.

As soon as the demands for the wholesale removal of those of Japanese ancestry surfaced in late December 1941, the JACL tried to frustrate the outcries. Among those clamoring for evacuation were governors and mayors on the Pacific Slope; the entire West Coast congressional delegation to Washington, D.C.; practically every newspaper, magazine, and radio station in the western states; most—if not all—farm and agricultural organizations; the various chambers of commerce and businessmen's associations; the American Legion and the Veterans of Foreign Wars; all labor unions except a few affiliated with the Congress of Industrial Organizations (CIO), and such special groups as the Native Sons and Daughters of the Golden West.

The JACL was far too weak in terms of membership, finances, staff, and public and political influence to be effective against the combination of events and individuals and organizations arrayed against it. Too few non-Japanese along the West Coast, including the overwhelming majority of Christian ministers and members of their congregations, protested at all. The rest of the country ignored what was happening to the civil, property, and human rights of Japanese Americans in the four westernmost states (Washington, Oregon, California, and Arizona).

On February 19, 1942, President Franklin D. Roosevelt signed Executive Order No. 9066, authorizing the secretary of war, or any military commander designated by him, to establish "military areas" and to exclude therefrom "any and all persons." On March 2, 1942, General John L. DeWitt, Commanding General of the Western Defense Command, by authority of the secretary of war, issued Public Proclamation No. 1. This designated the western half of California, Oregon, and Washington, and the southern third of Arizona as a military area, and it stipulated that all Japanese, both alien and non-alien, would eventually be removed from that military area.

"Military necessity" was the excuse used to justify this unprecedented action against native-born citizens and their resident alien parents who could not become naturalized citizens by law. It was done without trial or hearing in court, or even the formality of specific charges citing crimes or misconduct on the part of the prospective evacuees.

Thus, in the days after the presidential order authorizing evacuation, the JACL not only had to take care of almost all of the needs of every Japanese American community, but it also had to decide just what realistic alternatives there were for those of Japanese ancestry and which of these alternatives should be taken for the good of the minority as a whole. At the time the JACL was nothing more than a voluntary civic and educational association. It had been in existence nationally for less than twelve years. It had no paid staff except one untried national executive and a few local helpers working mostly on a part-time basis in the larger metropolitan areas, and it had absolutely no credentials or background for social services.

The decision to evacuate was not reached at a single meeting or a series of meetings of JACL officials when all of the facts, arguments, and options could have been carefully examined and discussed. Rather, because of the unique circumstances of those weeks, decision making was a kind of piecemeal operation, with most of those in responsible positions reaching their own conclusions, based upon the facts, rumors, and pressures that came to their attention. When one JACL official chanced across another, there was an exchange of ideas.

In spite of the seemingly haphazard method used, the fateful decision was not reached arbitrarily or capriciously, for all recognized their responsibilities. There was much too much at stake for the individuals concerned, not to mention the other 110,000 innocent people whose lives would be affected by whatever course might be taken. The consensus was developed by sober reflection, serious projections, and selfless disregard for personal consequences.

The awesome duty to recommend the basic course of action to be followed probably fell to one man more than any of the others. He was Saburo Kido, the national JACL president, who was then a practicing attorney in his late thirties. The decision also fell on me. I was the national JACL secretary and field executive and the first and only paid staff member in the history of the JACL. I was in my mid-twenties at the time: an untried, untrained youngster from Salt Lake City where there were few Japanese Americans and where the problems of the minority, if any, were quite different from those on the West Coast.

Nevertheless, since there were no others to assume the responsibilities, we did the best we could. Whenever there was an opportunity, Kido and I would discuss what course JACL should take in connection with the evacuation orders. Our discussions, of course, were based upon the facts as we knew them at that time, on the rumors that were called to our attention, and on the seemingly never-ending meetings which we held with government officials and army officers of all ranks.

Even after all these years, I still remember how wise and

statesmanlike Kido was. He had compassion for all the evacuees and a special sensitivity for the future of the young. What, then, were some of the considerations that led us to conclude that cooperation with the army in our own removal and eventual detention was our only sane and safe course? To begin with, both of us were very much aware of the racist, anti-Japanese history of the Pacific Coast, particularly California. Anti-Japanese sentiment, often wrapped in the cloak of patriotism, became so powerful that in 1924 it was able to persuade the Congress, against the wishes of President Calvin Coolidge and the State Department, to enact the infamous Japanese Exclusion Act together with the now thoroughly discredited National Origins Quota System. For a few short years, this racist ''victory'' against the so-called Yellow Peril softened anti-Japanese bigotry. But, with the great economic depression of the 1930s, when unemployment reached unprecedented numbers, the fact that Japanese Americans managed to stay off relief rolls infuriated many Caucasians. Toward the close of that decade, as the Japanese imperialists launched their military adventure against China, jingoists and warmongers joined the racists in a persecution of the Japanese Americans in their midst.

Then came the war, ignited by the attack of the Japanese militarists on Pearl Harbor. Navy wives and others, repatriated from Hawaii immediately after December 7, 1941, returned to the mainland with stories of espionage and sabotage committed by the Japanese American population before, during, and after the attack. They told of arrow-like marks cut in the sugar cane fields pointing to military installations, of Honolulu high school rings worn by the attacking Japanese airmen, and of Japanese Americans driving their trucks across highways to delay military personnel from reporting for duty during the attack.

Although these tales were rumors that were later proved unfounded, we were not informed of the truth until we were already in the War Relocation Authority (WRA) Centers, bitterly called concentration camps, American-style. Indeed, when members of the so-called Tolan Committee interrogated us in San Francisco in late February 1942, they repeated these rumors and demanded an explanation of such activities.

We were also aware that the governors of all twelve western states, with the sole exception of Ralph Carr of Colorado, had warned the army that they could not be responsible for the safety of the evacuees. They said that if the Japanese Americans were dangerous to the security of the Pacific Coast, they were equally dangerous to their respective jurisdictions. Mayors and public officials, except for Mayor Harry Cain of Tacoma, Washington, insisted upon the immediate removal of all the Japanese in their communities. Mayor Fletcher Bowron of Los Angeles was particularly vehement on this score although he apologized years later for his un-American and unconstitutional demands in 1942. All of the major newspapers except the *San Francisco Chronicle* editorially called upon the government to immediately evacuate and incarcerate the Japanese "for at least the duration" of the war.

Several caravans of trucks and automobiles, filled with Japanese Americans who were acting upon General DeWitt's suggestion that they "voluntarily" leave their homes and possessions in the military area in California, were stopped at gunpoint. Many of the trucks and cars were overturned, and everyone was forced to return to the homes from which they had departed only a few hours earlier.

There were rumors of vigilantism and arson, brutal attacks on individuals, and mob violence against Japanese American communities in some of the rural agricultural regions. The violence was no doubt aggravated by newspaper reports of unidentified planes flying over Los Angeles, lights seen near Santa Barbara on the California coast signaling enemy submarines offshore, and arsenals of weapons and ammunition found by the FBI in many Japanese American homes.

To my mind, however, the most damaging testimony was advanced by Earl Warren, then California's state attorney general. He had maps prepared showing that Japanese Americans

Mike Masaoka, who, along with other young Nisei leaders of the JACL, urged Japanese Americans to cooperate in evacuation and relocation.

While hundreds watched from an overpass, Japanese American families were marched to a train in Seattle for the trip to an assembly camp.

owned land near many military and naval installations. He furnished evidence that many Japanese Americans attended Japanese language schools, and he said that perhaps half of the Japanese population were members of the Buddhist faith. Warren charged also that the American-born citizen was more dangerous than his alien parents. Since even then Warren was thought to be a moderate in his attitudes toward other groups and in his outlook on legal issues, his official position was devastating in its influence on people who otherwise might have come to the defense of the constitutional rights of those of Japanese ancestry.

All these incidents, and considerably more, added up to the climate of public opinion against the Japanese in the spring of 1942.

Kido and I, along with a number of other invited Nisei leaders met with California Governor Culbert Olson in Sacramento. The governor warned us that evacuation and detention were imminent. He called upon us to volunteer to go to state-controlled labor camps from which some of us would return each day to harvest our own fields or other farmlands. The money we earned would go into the state treasury! We were informed from time to time of other schemes under which racists would supervise our incarceration and control our activities as laborers—regardless of our experience, education, and excellence in the professions.

As a last effort to prevent the evacuation, some members of the JACL volunteered to serve in combat against the Japanese enemy in the Pacific. But we were turned down summarily and without thanks.

Kido and I often discussed whether one or both of us should not violate the curfew or travel restrictions imposed by the Western Defense Command and test the constitutionality of the military orders. But we eventually rejected such an alternative since we would not have been able to be with the people during their evacuation and detention and would not share their sufferings and privations and indignities. Moreover, as an attorney,

Kido realized that it would take months and perhaps years before such constitutional challenges could be settled by the highest courts. In the meantime, the evacuees would be removed and jailed. Therefore, the two of us agreed that it would be our fate to remain among the prospective evacuees and to try to provide the necessary leadership as best we could. At the same time, we knew of several others who were willing to deliberately violate the curfew and travel restrictions, so we were confident that in time there would be a constitutional test of the issues at hand. We wondered, though, whether in time of war the courts would contradict the commander in chief and his military commanders in their efforts to ''protect'' the nation from possible invasion, as General DeWitt once claimed in the weeks following the attack on Pearl Harbor.

Both Kido and I were aware from word given us by the military and others that the army at one time was considering the removal and detention of only the enemy alien Japanese. These would be the Issei, who had been lawfully admitted into the United States but denied by federal statute the opportunity to become citizens through naturalization. By definition of law and through no fault of their own, they were enemy aliens. These were our parents, and their removal would not only separate family units but might also leave the aged and the infirm at the mercy of whatever fate awaited them in the camps. For these reasons, the JACL decided to object to the arbitrary separation of families, even though we knew that some of the more independent Nisei would denounce us for that decision. I now doubt that the JACL's beliefs concerning the integrity of the family unit had any bearing on the final military decision, for more and more people were demanding the complete removal of aliens and citizens alike.

About this time, we were beginning to wonder about the justification for evacuation on the grounds of military necessity. At first, General DeWitt had designated only the western half of the three Pacific Coast states and the southern third of Arizona as the military area from which military necessity required our removal. He had invited those of Japanese background to voluntarily leave this area and to relocate anywhere outside the designated zone. Many, including Kido's family, left their homes and relocated in the eastern half of California. Then, without any advance warning, General DeWitt arbitrarily added the eastern half of California to the military area from which all Japanese Americans were to be excluded. Thus, these evacuees were forced to undergo two evacuation programs: one voluntary and the other involuntary.

About this time, we were also told that the Japanese Americans in Hawaii would not be relocated on the mainland. In 1942 they constituted about a third of the total population of the islands, while we made up less than 1 percent of the total West Coast populace. Hawaii was some three thousand miles nearer to Japan than were the three westernmost states and had actually been under direct military attack. If military necessity dictated our evacuation and detention, what about the Japanese Americans in the Territory of Hawaii?

In the beginning, our wholesale removal and exclusion was demanded because of the fear of espionage or sabotage. Late in February 1942, federal intelligence agencies officially disclosed that before, during, and after December 7, 1941, no person of Japanese origin on the continental mainland had been convicted of either of these crimes. At this point, however, the army and such influential persons as Earl Warren and Walter Lippmann developed the curious doctrine that the actual absence of any espionage or sabotage was even more ominous than widespread treasonable activity. The Japanese Americans, it was alleged, were so well organized and disciplined that they were only waiting for an invasion by the enemy. Then they would rise up to support the Japanese invader.

Finally, it was argued that Japanese Americans had to be evacuated and placed in concentration camps in order to protect them from possible mob action by angry non-Japanese. In other words, the army resorted to the ''protective custody'' concept to justify our ultimate removal and incarceration.

Where was the "military necessity" in all this? These actions clearly revealed the racism behind our wartime mistreatment. But what could the JACL have done to overcome racism, when the government, the army, and practically the total population of the West Coast were all united in the demand for evacuation and exclusion?

Even now I remember well the government's presentation of the basic problem to the JACL. We met in early March 1942, with a group of special emissaries from Washington, D. C. They informed us bluntly that the decision had been made to evacuate all persons of Japanese descent, aliens and citizens alike, from the western half of California, Oregon, and Washington, and the southern third of Arizona. We would first be detained in Wartime Civilian Control Administration (WCCA) assembly camps in racetracks and fairgrounds. Later, we would be taken to the War Relocation Authority (WRA) camps then being constructed by the army in interior wastelands in California, Arizona, Idaho, Utah, Colorado, Wyoming, and Arkansas.

We were urged to cooperate with the army in that removal and detention program, even though it would mean personal sacrifices and suffering and considerable loss of property. If we failed to cooperate, the army would put its contingency plan into operation, and we would be forcibly ejected and incarcerated.

Having been forewarned that the decision had been made to order a mass evacuation, we were not surprised by the announcements. And, since we had discussed the JACL's leadership position on the issue of cooperation with the army, the ultimate decision itself was not difficult to make. We did, however, refuse to commit ourselves at that meeting and requested time to confer with our fellow JACL leaders. But we all felt that we had no alternative to cooperation. Resistance was suicidal.

Our only friend in Washington who might have been able to convince the president and the secretary of war that the evacuation was both unconstitutional and unnecessary was Attorney

General Francis Biddle, a noted civil libertarian. He had already capitulated to the military and political demand for total evacuation, however, even though Navy Intelligence and the FBI, as we learned later, opposed the mass evacuation as unnecessary and undesirable. Given the situation, how could we — with little or no influence — continue to "fight" and hope against evacuation?

Furthermore, we were led to believe that if we cooperated with the army in this mass movement, the army, the WRA, and the government would try to be as helpful and as humane as possible to the evacuees. Moreover, we feared the consequences if Japanese Americans refused to cooperate, and the army moved in with armed troops and even tanks to eject the people forcibly from their homes and properties. At a time when Japan was still on the offensive and apparently winning the war, we were afraid that the American people would consider us traitors and enemies of the war effort if we forced the army to take drastic action against us. This might forever place in jeopardy our future as United States citizens. As the involuntary trustees of the destiny of the Japanese Americans in this country, we felt that we could do no less than whatever was necessary to protect and preserve that future.

We were quite aware of the personal attitudes of some of the military personnel involved. General DeWitt, who would be in direct charge of any military action against the Japanese, had testified to a Senate Naval Affairs Subcommittee in words to this effect: "A Jap's a Jap. Blood is thicker than citizenship. And giving them a piece of paper to show their citizenship won't change that fact." Colonel Bendetsen, the director of the WCCA, who would supervise the initial movement out of the homes of the evacuees, was determined that any person who was as much as one-sixteenth Japanese, which was double the formula devised by Hitler for the Jews, should be evacuated as a Japanese alien or non-alien.

Probably even more pertinent to our decision to cooperate was the official war policy of the United States government at that time. The policy was to depict the Japanese as an enemy to be defeated at all costs. Therefore, official propaganda promoted the belief that the Japanese were barbarians who could not be trusted and who should be annihilated. Should the JACL give a doubting nation further excuse to confuse the identity of the Japanese enemy with the American of Japanese origin?

Suppose there might be blood shed on the streets of many Pacific Coast communities? We leaders of the JACL could not opt for such a grim and possibly genocidal alternative. With reluctant and heavy hearts, Kido and I joined in calling upon the JACL delegates to the National Emergency Council in San Francisco in mid-March 1942 to urge their members and others of Japanese ancestry in the prohibited zones to cooperate as best they could with the army. We said that they had to move from their homes to temporary assembly centers and then to what might become permanent relocation camps. There were some heated debates and some bitter comments. But, in the end, there was close to unanimity. With sad farewells, not knowing whether they would ever see each other again and weighed down by the decision to cooperate in what amounted to their own banishment and imprisonment, the delegates returned to their home districts to report on the JACL position.

Frankly, at that time, both Kido and I were quite surprised and pleased that there was practically no public outcry or challenge against the decision to cooperate with the army. We believed that such near total compliance indicated the general agreement of the evacuees that cooperation was indeed the proper arrangement under those tumultuous and threatening conditions.

Despite all that we had to suffer as suspect citizens of our own government, many besides myself must have hoped that if we demonstrated our belief in American ideals and objectives, the people of the United States would somehow more than make up for what we had sacrificed after the hate and hysteria of the war was over.

After more than twenty-five years in Washington, D. C., I

am convinced that our decision was the correct and proper one, and the only one that could have been reached at that time by responsible and reasonable people.

I still cannot adequately describe those emotions we felt —fear and fright, anger and helplessness, and hope and faith in spite of frustrations and tears. But I am hopeful that the facts and events as I recall them now will provide an insight into why we in the JACL leadership came to the decision that we did in relation to the 1942 mass evacuation and detention of 110,000 human beings of Japanese ancestry.

In checking testimony to congressional committees and to presidential commissions, I have observed how many Americans have called for corrective, remedial, and even beneficial legislation for those of Japanese ancestry because of the unprecedented wartime cooperation shown by the Japanese Americans. I cannot even count the many times over the last twenty-five years that members of the Congress and officials of the various administrations, especially those from the Pacific Coast, have introduced and voted for legislation and regulations that have been most helpful and beneficial to Japanese Americans. I am often reminded that the Japanese experience of 1942 involving wholesale evacuation and detention remains to prick the American conscience. The cooperative spirit and actions of the evacuees themselves shamed many Americans in later years when they learned of that travesty on American justice and constitutional guarantees.

In any event, because of the Japanese American wartime cooperation, the WRA was administered by able and sympathetic officials in a most humane manner under the circumstances, especially considering the continuing racism of many West Coasters who demanded the deportation of all Japanese after the war. Due to this cooperation, the president and the army agreed to the formation of what became the 442nd Regimental Combat Team and the use of Nisei combat intelligence troops in the Pacific. The WRA policy and program encouraged student evacuees to leave the centers to continue their higher education

Waiting to be taken away from her home, a little girl holds on to her doll.

and qualified evacuees to seek housing and employment outside the centers. Many worked in jobs and professions that had been closed to them prior to World War II on the West Coast.

Since World War II, Congress has enacted laws that provide naturalization and immigration opportunities not only for the Japanese but also for all who lawfully enter this country for permanent residence. It has authorized partial compensation for economic losses suffered in the evacuation and exclusion era and has granted statehood to Hawaii, where a large percentage of the population is of Japanese descent. It has extended civil and human rights to all Americans, without regard to race, color, creed, or national origin.

The courts, in turn, have handed down decision after decision defining the rights and opportunities for those of Japanese background and others previously denied justice under the law. Over the years, Japanese Americans have gained assurances of "equality and opportunity under law."

Altogether, it is estimated that some five hundred pre-war laws and ordinances that restricted the lives of those of Japanese ancestry in this country, aliens and citizens alike, are no longer valid and effective. Indeed, it is often said that never before have those of Japanese origin been more respected and able to enjoy the rights, privileges, and opportunities of American citizenship than today. In these and many other ways, the fateful JACL decision, more than thirty years ago, to urge cooperation in the wartime evacuation and detention of the Japanese on the Pacific Coast is vindicated time and time again.

To all of those people who may, in other times, challenge that decision, it can only be said that any review of that determination must be made in the context of 1942. It must be made with the knowledge that because of that cooperative demonstration, those of Japanese ancestry are now in a position to inquire about the rightness and the consequences of that course of action decided more than three decades ago in what was a very different and difficult period in U.S. history.

5.
Internment

Puyallup Fairgrounds is the home of the Western Washington State Fair, popularly known as the Puyallup Fair, where farmers and 4-H Club members proudly display their products and livestock and vie for blue and gold ribbons. People congregate here to see a horse show and chat gaily while browsing through the exhibits. The youngsters spend their time eating popcorn, hot dogs, and hamburgers; drinking coke; and riding on the merry-go-round and the ferris wheel. A carnival atmosphere prevails in normal times.

But 1942 was different. That year, the Puyallup Fair site was taken over by the army and converted into an assembly center to imprison Japanese from the surrounding area. Puyallup Assembly Center was one of fifteen temporary concentration camps used until the army could build permanent camps.

In the Puyallup Center, the question on everyone's mind was: what will they do to us now? Some Issei truly felt they were being rushed to camp for mass execution. Many wept in silence for their children who had been raised to become good American citizens and who had done nothing to shame the United States.

The Puyallup camp was euphemistically named Camp Harmony. It was set up like a prison camp. One Nisei describes the area in which he lived, originally a parking lot, as having two watchtowers and floodlights between the barracks. The residents were guarded by armed soldiers. Another Nisei remem-

Seattle Japanese evacuees eat their first meal in one of the mess halls at Puyallup Assembly Center.

bers the flimsy barracks and the lack of privacy. The partitions separating the living units within the barracks did not reach the ceiling so that conversations could be heard halfway down the length of the building.

Occasionally, the Japanese Americans had Caucasian visitors, who brightened their lives for a moment. Some brought refreshments; wives visited their husbands. Friends and neighbors of some interned families did not let the war alter their relations with them. These visitors went out of their way to help the families with words of comfort and continued friendship.

Life for most Japanese Americans during this period, however, is best described by the dark words of Mrs. Miyo Uchiyama:[10]

The thing that really hit most of us was the lack of privacy. There was no privacy whatsoever. You could see daylight in between slats of the buildings. A good day for Peeping Toms if there were any. No closets. Just a potbelly stove for each family in one room. I really felt sorry for some of the teenagers, especially the shy ones. Some couldn't take it. I recall one of the girls lost her mind.

For most Japanese, it was a time of discomfort and a time for thinking about how they got there. That period was to last from May to September, when the people at Puyallup were transferred to Minidoka, Idaho, one of ten permanent relocation centers. Having received their basic training at Puyallup, the Japanese Americans were mentally and physically prepared to meet the bigger and better concentration camp in September.

Mrs. Uchiyama recalls the transfer as a painful experience:

I remember going by bus to the center of Puyallup to board the train. They had people haul and load our baggage. That was the first time I really began to realize what would happen to us. The thought came to my mind, and I was practically in tears, ''Will we come back?'' And I think it was the only time it really hit me . . . .

The camp wasn't ready by the time the residents arrived, but the buildings were fairly substantial army-type barracks. They were far from comfortable, though. Mrs. Uchiyama comments on the problem of dust, one which persisted for about six months: ''We could sit in a room, and the dust would be so thick we couldn't see the other wall. And the only way we could find comfort to even breathe was to throw blankets over our heads and hope that the dust wouldn't seep through.'' The barracks were unheated, and there was even a scarcity of hot water for doing laundry and bathing.

Home for one married couple was appallingly small, about twelve feet by twelve feet. For furniture there were only two wooden cots and a big black cast-iron stove set in a bed of sand.

There were windows on either side of the room, and one light bulb hung from the center of the ceiling. There were no chairs, tables, benches, or closets. This couple's first efforts were to make the place habitable. They had to resort to stealing lumber, plasterboard, and fiberboard. In a short time, they had made essential furniture and built closets. The meals were sufficient, although they were highly starchy and completely dull.

Under the supervision of the WRA, the Japanese Americans formed their own staff for running the camp. Their pay ranged from eight to twelve dollars per month for the unskilled, and from twelve to nineteen dollars for the skilled. The residents were given more latitude in their activities than previously. This change in the operation of the camp came because of the shift from a military authority (the WCCA) to a civilian authority (the WRA). The purpose of the WRA was not to keep the people under armed guard, but rather to "detain" them temporarily prior to relocation out of the center into civilian life.

The center had such service and recreational facilities as a post office, gasoline station, canteen, library, social hall, ball field, church, theater, and "swimming hole." There were also schools for the children.

One of the busiest places in the center was the canteen. A cooperative had been organized, and one could order through catalogues things like clothes, shoes, and cosmetics—things that helped one to feel more like an individual in spite of the fact that one was in a concentration camp. But on twelve or nineteen dollars a month, there was not much anyone could afford.

One person who was sent to the relocation center in Granada, Colorado, wrote: "I'll never forget the vast loneliness I felt when I looked upon the hills of Granada, Colorado, and detected rows and rows of barracks. The Issei wept openly, many of them wondering if they would live through this. And many did not."

Rohwer Relocation Center was situated in the lowlands of

Young volunteer workers at Granada Relocation Center in Amache, California, spend their first Sunday afternoon in the barracks.

A ninth-grade class at Rohwer Relocation Center in Mc-Gehee, Arkansas.

Children heading for their barracks after school at the Manzanar Relocation Center in Manzanar, California.

Evacuees picking cucumbers at a farm near the Gila, Arizona, relocation center.

Arkansas. A former internee there remembers the uniformity and regimentation vividly.

You had to line up for this, line up for that. And it was rather frustrating to us that freedom was only about one-hundred yards away from our camp. I can still see the road where occasionally we'd see a man leisurely driving an old mule-powered wagon. We couldn't even have the liberty to go up to see that road or to cross it to see what was beyond that.

A California man, Dr. Kenneth Ozawa, remembers completing the fifth, sixth, seventh, and part of his eighth school year at Topaz Relocation Center in Utah. He also recalls the armed soldiers stationed in towers, and the barbed wire. Blue stars hung in the windows of barracks that housed relatives of Japanese Americans serving in the war; gold stars hung for those killed in action.

Ozawa has never forgotten one spring day at Topaz. James H. Wakasa, sixty-two, decided he wanted to walk toward the outer fence to pick some flowers. It was to be his last walk; an MP sentry shot and killed him. Wakasa had failed to heed four warnings from the sentries in the watch towers. Whether he did not hear the warnings or deliberately set out to get himself killed, no one will ever know. Not long after, the army removed the sentries from the towers.

At least two thousand residents attended the outdoor funeral for Wakasa. The camp was in an uproar following the shooting, and morale was low for nearly a year. It is tragic that Wakasa was slain by a man who represented the military organization he himself had once served. Wakasa had been a civilian instructor in cooking at Camp Dodge, Iowa, during World War I.

In 1971, Congress repealed the Emergency Detention Act of 1950, more popularly referred to as Title II, Internal Security Act of 1950. Title II threatened all Americans with the provision for detention of such persons as there is reasonable ground to believe ''will engage in, or probably will conspire with others to

Wintertime at the Minidoka, Idaho, relocation center.

engage in, acts of espionage or sabotage'' in the event of invasion, declaration of war, or insurrection in the United States in aid of a foreign enemy.

The national Japanese American Citizens League saw in Title II the possibility that another segment of the American society might be arbitrarily herded into so-called ''relocation centers'' without trial. The JACL was in the forefront of those advocating the repeal of Title II. Supporting the JACL position in the federal government were two members of the much decorated 442nd Regimental Combat Team of World War II fame— Senator Daniel Inouye and Representative Spark Matsunaga, both from Hawaii.

Newspapers, churches, the American Civil Liberties Union, social workers, ethnic groups, labor unions, and many other organizations supported the JACL campaign. It is interesting that some of the strongest support for repeal of the act came from the California press.

An elderly woman picks up bits of coal to keep her stove burning in the Minidoka, Idaho, camp.

Then there was the letter from Earl Warren, former chief justice of the United States Supreme Court, in which he stated that Title II is not in the American tradition. This was a big change from his stand before the evacuation. In fairness to Warren, it should be said that he, as governor of California in 1945–46, was responsible for the generally orderly return of evacuees to his state. Later, as chief justice, Warren achieved an outstanding record in the field of human rights and constitutional liberties. These actions may have been Warren's way of making up for his misjudgment during a period of wartime hysteria.

In December 1971, President Richard M. Nixon sent to the JACL committee one of the pens used to sign the law repealing Title II of the Internal Security Act of 1950. Along with the pen, the president sent the following letter:

> In September of this year, I signed into law the repeal of the Emergency Detention Act of 1950. This, of course, had special meaning for many Americans of Japanese descent, and because of the many contributions you have made as an outstanding leader in the Nisei community, including your efforts in the repeal of Title II, I am pleased to present you with one of the pens used in the signing of this measure. [11]

Although the United States has taken steps to ensure that another mass evacuation will not occur, the 1944 ruling by the United States Supreme Court, upholding the legality of the evacuation based solely upon race, still stands. We cannot yet consider a repetition of this mass evacuation—with a minority group as the victim—an impossibility.

In June 1967, a talk was given by Dr. Harry H. L. Kitano at the University of California as a part of a symposium entitled: *It Happened Here: The Japanese Evacuation of 1942*. Dr. Kitano hypothesized that, given certain conditions, genocide or extinction could have occurred as a final step in the action, out of racial prejudice. If Japanese forces had actually invaded the United States mainland or if their bombers had destroyed

American cities with high casualties to civilians, then Japanese Americans might have been slaughtered for the "good of Americans."

Dr. Kitano, a professor of social welfare and sociology, questioned the "villain theories" which attribute evil acts solely to sick or disturbed individuals. Instead, said Kitano, acts such as the internment of the Japanese are frequently done as part of a bureaucratic process. Before such actions are initiated, the group in question has been discriminated against and segregated by the general populace. "The isolated, powerless group is the target of rumors and propaganda and because they are set apart and are the recipients of negative attitudes, officials can now initiate popular actions against them. Instead of being viewed as humans, they are likened to animals." Given a key event, such as the attack on Pearl Harbor, normal constitutional rights may be withheld.

"Once the process is set into motion," Kitano concluded, "the final solution is not too distant."[12]

Those who believe they are immune to that sort of cruelty should stop and reflect on Dr. Kitano's remarks. It could happen.

6.

Japanese Americans in Combat

Although the official purpose of internment was to separate Japanese Americans from a country at war, the war came to the camps. On January 28, 1943, the War Department reopened its doors to Americans of Japanese descent for military service. The 442nd Regimental Combat Team was made up of mainland Japanese Americans.

When the Army decided to accept Nisei volunteers, the response from those interned was, naturally enough, not wholly favorable. Only about 6 percent of all the eligible Nisei males enrolled as volunteers, and over one-quarter of the Nisei refused to answer questions as to their loyalties. Months of questioning and internment had angered many of the men. When potential volunteers prepared to register for military service, many asked whether or not rejection from such service would affect their families and themselves. As a result, restrictions on the volunteers themselves were eased.

A year after the Army began accepting Nisei enlistees and after the Nisei began their impressive performance in Europe, the Selective Service system announced that Nisei would be compelled to perform military service despite the conditions of internment. Even after swearing allegiance to the United States, Nisei inductees were still treated as enemy aliens. Individual Nisei who refused to comply with draft procedures were convicted of criminal evasion and sent to prison. The evacuation of Japanese Americans was not seen as an invasion of constitutional rights, and so it did not provide a sufficient reason for refusal to serve in the army. By 1947, however, those who had been imprisoned for violation of the Selective Service Act had received pardons and were restored to the privileges of citizenship.

How did other Americans react to the army's change of this policy? West Coast newspapers generally favored the army's action in reopening military service to citizens of Japanese ancestry.

The editor of the *San Francisco Chronicle* commented that "there are encouraging beginnings toward a more rational treatment of Americans of Japanese ancestry." [13] The Santa Rosa, California, *Press Democrat* said that the idea to form an all-Japanese-American fighting unit, with its own officers, infantry, medical personnel, and mechanized force "was perfectly sound." The *Press Democrat* went on:

> The surprising thing about it all is that such a plan had not been in operation long ago. Such a fighting unit would not necessarily be sent to fight the Japanese. It could be sent to face the Italians and Germans. It could, with good effect, be given a small sector in Tunisia, or any other battlefront.... A move of this kind would end forever any American talk about the Japanese in relocation settlements being pampered. [14]

In 1944, the 442nd Regimental Combat Team went to Italy to join the 100th Infantry Battalion which was made up of Nisei national guardsmen from Hawaii. When news of their heroic deeds shot back across the Atlantic to the states and into the camps, and even into the far-flung battlefields of the Pacific, the government eased its grip on the interned Japanese. It was a moment of joy experienced by those Caucasians who, despite "Jap-lovers" ephithets, had kept their faith in the loyalty of the Japanese Americans.

General Mark W. Clark, Commanding General of the Fifth Army in the Italian campaign, stated: "I am convinced that no

Men of the 442nd Regimental Combat Team cheer for their side at a baseball game during basic training at Camp Shelby, Mississippi.

wartime commander ever had at his disposal a finer body of fighting men than the 442nd.... Their sacrifice in terms of loss of lives, wounds, and general privation cannot be repaid by mere words, but their deeds have won the sincere admiration of Americans.''[15]

Endorsements also came from individuals like Dillon S. Myer, director of the War Relocation Authority, Senator Elbert Thomas of Utah, and Milton Eisenhower, former director of the WRA. Theater audiences throughout the nation applauded newsreel clippings of Nisei training for combat duty at Camp Shelby, Mississippi.

There were other Americans, however, who did not seem happy about Japanese Americans helping in the war effort. As the Army began recruiting Nisei volunteers for a Japanese American combat team, opposition arose from such diverse sources as the Idaho State Legislature and the Native Daughters of the Golden West.

The men of the 442nd wore a shoulder patch with a torch for

the centerpiece. It was a torch that was to light the way to military glory, culminating in the 442nd being acclaimed as the most decorated unit for its size and length of service in the history of the United States Armed Forces.

In a letter written in 1945, Secretary of War Robert P. Patterson commented:

> Through the bitter fighting in Italy and later as a part of the forces which struck at the German Armies through Southern France, the battle skill, cool bravery and individual fortitude of these men became legendary to comrades and enemy alike.

> Soon the men who performed them—the survivors of this gallant unit—will return to their homes after receiving the honor and acclaim of their Commander-in-Chief [President Truman] and other leaders of their country. They go back as honored veterans to Hawaii, to the Western States and other communities which sent them to battle. Their friends and neighbors and all the citizens of the communities they represent share the pride in their heroic achievements. These men are heroes. No American will forget it....[16]

While the Japanese Americans were stationed mainly in Europe, there were some men fighting Japan in the Pacific. Reports about these men came to light only in fragments. One reason for this was the fear of reprisals against relatives in Japan of Nisei serving America. By 1944, however, the public was given a better look at the Japanese Americans fighting the war against Japan. Most of these men served in ATIS (the Allied Translator and Interpreter Section) or G-2, as it was better known.

A lieutenant interviewed in 1944 about Nisei serving in the Pacific said:

> These Japanese are Americans—American-born Nisei and soldiers in the U.S. Army, who have been serving

with the Marine detachments in the Pacific Islands and otherwise providing the leatherneck fighters with the benefit of their knowledge of enemy ways. They have the respect of the Marines because they are good American soldiers, and we realize the risks they are exposed to in event they are captured by the enemy.[17]

The same lieutenant later reminisced:

As it was, these boys had a tough time of it. Each one of them had been captured eight or nine times—by our own men. One day two of them were seized while standing in a Marine show line, in their dungarees. It got to the point where finally, for their own protection, we had to detail a Marine to accompany them wherever they went. The men took it in good spirit.

Nisei GI specialists handled two million enemy documents during World War II, and were extremely important in dealing with linguistic problems. "We would still be at war with

Hiroshi Miyamura, a member of the 442nd combat team in World War II and recipient of the Medal of Honor in the Korean War, receives a key to the city from Seattle's mayor.

Japan if it was not for the Nisei intelligence work,'' said one former officer.[18] Their combat record paralleled their brilliant linguistic record. More than 180 received awards ranging from the Bronze Star to the Distinguished Service Cross, while some 125 additional personnel were cited by division and brigade commanders.

Sergeant Frank Hachiya, of Hood River, Oregon, became one of the great Nisei war heroes of World War II in the Pacific. He volunteered for combat duty while he was at Minidoka Relocation Center in Idaho. After being graduated from the Military Intelligence Service Language School, he was assigned to serve in the Pacific for undercover work behind enemy lines. When the invasion of Leyte Island in the Philipines began, Sergeant Hachiya started to crawl from behind the Japanese lines toward the landing United States troops. Mistaken for an enemy, he was mortally wounded by the invading American soldiers. Nevertheless, this Nisei soldier managed to crawl far enough forward to lay at an American officer's feet a complete map of the Japanese defenses for Leyte. Without a question, Sergeant Hachiya's courageous deed saved the lives of hundreds of American soldiers. A grateful nation awarded him the Distinguished Service Cross posthumously. Ironically, in Hood River, Oregon, the American Legion had at that time removed the names of Nisei servicemen, including Hachiya, from its community honor roll of servicemen. The names were later restored with a comment by the national American Legion commander that Legionnaires are ''honest enough to admit a mistake, big enough to correct it.''

Why did the Nisei go through such hell when their parents, brothers, and sisters were imprisoned behind barbed wire? When their families' belongings were abandoned, given away, or sold for almost nothing? When their loyalty was questioned with insults, indignities, and innuendo? The Japanese Americans had to weather the climate of distrust. For some of the Nisei, the war became a personal fight to erase doubts existing over their loyalty.

On April 30, 1943, a Nisei en route to Camp Shelby, Mississippi, to train for overseas duty with the 442nd, sent a letter to his father in which he recalled his father's reaction to the bombing of Pearl Harbor.

You turned pale when you heard the news. For days after, you were silent in your misery. Japan was the country of your birth, but America, the country of your choice. From that day you ceased speaking of Japan. Out of this treachery grew our misery.

In the spring of the following year, we were forced to evacuate to the relocation centers. It was a bitter blow to me. I, a citizen, with a brother already serving in the Army, must evacuate, and I could not understand why the German and the Italian aliens were not included. I had had an unbounding faith in the justice of this nation, but she in return had placed me behind barbed wires like any enemy alien. I was stricken with bitterness, and bitter was my denunciation of the government for this apparent discrimination.

Then you comforted me and slowly withdrew the sting of bitterness as you did many years ago when mother passed away. I could not understand at the time why you should attempt to restore my faith in the government which had never given you the right of citizenship and now by evacuation had made you again penniless. But I did not realize the love you bore for this country, made more dear because here it was that mother had died and had been laid to rest: "Where your treasure is there will your heart be also."

How clearly I remember your words of consolation now even as I write this letter. Wisely you said: "It is for the best. For the good of many a few must suffer. This is your sacrifice, accept it as such, and you will no longer be bitter."

A military funeral for a member of the 442nd regiment, killed in action in the Italian campaign in World War II.

At a flag ceremony held in the Minidoka, Idaho, relocation center, parents accept a flag for their son, a member of the 442nd regiment, who was killed in action.

I listened to your words and the bitterness left me. A despised alien without citizenship, you showed me what it means to be a citizen. That I have retained my faith through this trying period and emerged what I am, a loyal American citizen, I owe to your understanding. When the time came for enlistment, I was ready, my faith and loyalty restored, stronger, firmer, unwavering; I volunteered. And tonight as the train carries me farther and farther from you, it also seemed to carry me back over the years of our happy life, recalling to me those days when we were five, then four, then three, and now you are only two.

There is an old Japanese, or is it a Chinese, saying that a man must weep thrice ere his span of life is done, or words to this effect. I do not know whether this is true or not, but I have already seen you weep twice, once in sorrow and once in joy, and if this be true and it is predestined that you must weep again, then Dad, let it be for me in glory, for the victory that shall surely be mine. God bless you, Dad, and keep you until this happy day.[19]

George Sawada went to Italy as a member of the Red Cross detachment assigned to the 442nd Regimental Combat Team in May 1943. On July 5, 1943, George volunteered for front line duty. He was shot and killed by an enemy sniper the same evening.

The classic Hawaiian crapshooter's expression "Go for broke" was the motto of the Nisei 442nd Regimental Combat Team as it served in the United States Army, and "shoot the works" was what these Japanese Americans did during World War II. They fought for the country they had come to know as their own. Like many other Americans fighting beside them, they were willing to risk their lives for the country they loved.

7.
Intermarriage: The Postwar Bride

As the generations of Japanese in America pass from the Issei, who came here filled with the traditions of the mother country, on through the Nisei and Sansei and even the fourth-generation Yonsei, the ties to Japan must naturally change if not weaken. One important cause for the breaking up of an ethnic group is interracial marriage. Might we someday have a complete mixing of races—a loss of Japanese physical characteristics as well as affinity with Japanese ways?

This chapter will first take a look at the effect of interracial marriages on the Japanese American community. It will then glance at the problems which have faced that group of soldiers who married in Japan and returned with their brides to this country.

For centuries in Japan, families were responsible for arranging the marriages of their children, often with the aid of a third party, an intermediary known as a *baishakunin*. This third party in the marriage settlement existed to rid the families of the possibility of a difficult interaction and so enable them to preserve a proper form of conduct toward one another. For his efforts, the baishakunin was given a token of appreciation.

With the development of photography, families often exchanged pictures, particularly when there was some distance separating them. Since the Issei men were still closely tied with Japan and its tradition, they often exchanged pictures with women there and had their marriages arranged by the baishakunin. Exclusionists on the West Coast likened this to the system of mail-order brides. They called these women "picture brides," and condemned them on moral grounds. The exclusionists, needless to say, did not take into account the Japanese tradition, or the care with which the search for a partner was undertaken.

With the second generation, the Nisei, the marriage arrangement changed somewhat. Nisei married Nisei, but in selecting a mate, the Nisei were more independent than the Issei. They seldom requested a baishakunin to arrange a marriage, and those who did so were ridiculed by most other Nisei. But certain traditions, such as the caste system, were still important. Victims of the caste system were the *Etas* (outsiders), who were frowned on as mates for matrimony because they were descendants of butchers and tanners. The Japanese Buddhist society was very much opposed to those who made a living slaughtering animals. The Issei knew who the Etas were, and that knowledge hurt Nisei boys and girls whose parents happened to carry the social stigma of being Etas. At the present time, however, the question of whether or not a person is of the Eta class happily appears to be dying with the gradual passing of the Issei from the Japanese community scene.

Intermarriages between Japanese men and white women occurred here and there among the Issei. They were the men who either didn't take time to write to Japan, or who had lost contact with the Japanese American community. These were definitely exceptions, though. During and after World War II, the number of intermarriages climbed noticeably among the Nisei. More often than not, it was a result of attending public schools or universities.

The Issei never worried too much about their children dating and marrying. One reason, perhaps, was that the Japanese American community was still a "closed society." But as the Japanese move more and more freely into Western society, the Nisei parents face an entirely different situation. They see intimate social contacts with non-Japanese as threatening the cultural structure of their people. In general, Nisei parents seem to prefer that their children, the Sansei, marry persons of Japanese ancestry. After the Japanese, the Nisei parents next look to the Chinese, and then to the *hakujin* (white people) as suitable partners in marriage.

Since Nisei parents are eager for their children to meet and marry other Japanese, the Nisei from such places as Chicago often send their children to the West Coast to introduce them to eligible Japanese young people. Parents are often willing to go considerable distances for the sake of their children. But not all Nisei feel that they should dictate to their children whom they should date and marry. Studies done by sociologists and psychologists indicate that most Sansei do not feel as strongly as their parents about Japanese dating and Japanese marriages. Like their non-Japanese counterparts, these Sansei are much more liberal. There is visible evidence everywhere of interracial dating and interracial marriages.

In the fall of 1971, a Fresno State College sociologist said that the Japanese interracial marriage rate in Fresno County surpassed 50 percent in 1964 and has continued to rise ever since. The figure includes, however, not only marriage licenses issued to Sansei, but also to recent Japanese immigrants and, in all likelihood, to Nisei and Yonsei.[20]

The increase in interracial marriages between Japanese and non-Japanese brings up a speculation: if many of the states didn't have antimiscegenation laws, how many more Japanese would have intermarried? In California, for instance, whites were barred from marrying non-whites until 1948. It wasn't until 1967 that the United States Supreme Court lifted the barrier permitting persons to be married irrespective of race or color.

Despite the rise in interracial marriages, there continues to be—and according to experts in this field, there will probably always be — a hard core of people who insist on ethnic marriages. In one western city the Japanese population has greatly increased despite the fact that the Japanese are scattered throughout the city. Further, the 1970 United States census clearly shows a marked increase in Japanese population throughout the nation. Thus, while there has been some breaking down of tradition among the Japanese Americans, the complete assimilation of the Japanese group into Western society is not a likelihood.

The end of World War II and the legislation regarding soldiers' brides which followed thrust the first group of Japanese postwar brides into the Japanese American communities in 1948. The postwar brides came from the middle and lower classes. Among them were entertainers, dance hall hostesses, barmaids, and also some who worked for the Allied forces in Japan. Not too many came from families who were well-to-do, for they were not as brutally confronted with the question of survival in a war-torn country.

In the beginning, the postwar brides were welcomed with open arms. It was *"Yoku irrasshai-mashita!"* (It's nice you were able to come!) Many churches on the West Coast went out of their way to make the newcomers feel at home. Teas, get-together socials, and classes in American cooking, shopping, and customs were sponsored. In return, the talented among the postwar brides had the knowledge and skill to teach Japanese dancing, *koto* (harp), *shamisen* (lute), *ikebana* (flower arrangement), and even piano.

Misunderstandings and prejudices due to cultural and language differences soon arose and made life painfully difficult for the postwar brides and their husbands. As the reception cooled, the women began to assimilate on their own into the greater American society. The conflict in the Japanese community was a case of Japanese discriminating against Japanese.

The second wave of postwar brides made a mild splash in the Japanese communities about 1951–1952. Their presence was felt, but there was only a small concern for them. Most of these women somehow adjusted; those who didn't or couldn't cope with the difficulties vanished from the Japanese communities.

The more fortunate postwar brides were those whose husbands decided to pursue a livelihood in cities such as New York, Chicago, Los Angeles, or San Francisco, which are large enough to have a Japanese population and to carry Japanese food and Japanese goods. Postwar brides married to non-Japanese encountered other problems, among them the prejudices of their in-laws. In some cases, a husband's chances of promotion in employment might suffer because his wife happened to be Japanese. Homesickness has often plagued these postwar brides who yearn for Japanese people to talk to, Japanese food to eat, and the Japanese scenery and climate. Most Japanese women don't get divorces, however, unless their husbands initiate the proceedings because divorce is thought to be improper in Japanese culture.

Most postwar brides and their husbands, it appears, are resilient enough to withstand the onslaught of American society's subtle form of discrimination and prejudices. Most of the children of these marriages are flowing easily and gently into the American stream. In general, the mood of the 1970s is one of wide acceptance for them.

8.
Product of
Two Cultures

Culture in the Japanese American community has been passed from one generation to the next at the family dinner table, at a church social, at a convention, or at a Japanese language school. The more culture-conscious take private lessons; the others learn by observing their parents, brothers, sisters, relatives, and friends.

While the culture which the Japanese Americans have adopted is largely a blend of the Japanese and the American, it has been the Japanese culture that has sustained the Japanese when they venture outside their community. The knowledgeable outsider knows that Japanese culture cradles the delicate, the sensitive, the sophisticated way of life. This culture includes *chano-yu* (tea ceremony), *ikebana* (flower arrangement), *bonsai* (art of dwarfing trees), *odori* (dance), *origami* (paper folding), and judo, karate, sumo (wrestling), and *kendo* (fencing).

Harmonious human relations are especially important to the Japanese. This trait has been so admired by others that the Japanese are often described as the "model American minority." They are also respected for their ability to take in and adapt to new ideas. This is not merely imitation, for the Japanese have absorbed elements of other civilizations for centuries yet produced a culture distinctly Japanese. In the United States, the Japanese have learned to uphold many values cherished by middle-class Americans: success in school, in a career, and as a citizen. Principles such as justice, duty, responsibility, obligation, gratitude, loyalty, patience, perseverance, and self-restraint have been important in shaping Japanese behavior. Many of these Japanese behavioral norms strongly resemble American social values. While there is a similarity in the traditional standards guiding Japanese and Americans, however, the Japanese success in America has also been achieved by a partial sacrifice of their identity as Japanese to enable a wholehearted adoption of middle-class values.

As has been mentioned before in this book, the Japanese in America have tended to gather together in Japanese communities. They call these *Nihonmachi* (Japanese town). Here they can best maintain traditional Japanese customs. In addition, they have set up such businesses as barber shops, law firms, grocery stores, insurance agencies, drug stores, restaurants, and doctors' offices. Like many another struggling immigrant group, they place a high value on economic security. They build Buddhist and Christian churches, and they organize clubs which provide many activities—dances, conventions, picnics, dinners, and skating parties—to fill their social needs. They also celebrate Thanksgiving, Christmas, and New Year's Day, which have been borrowed from other Americans.

The Issei and the Kibei lean more toward Japanese traditions than do the Nisei. The *Kibei* are those Americans of Japanese ancestry who received their schooling in Japan. They are very Japanese in their mannerisms, speech, and attitudes. Many Nisei think of them as "different."

The most important holiday for the Japanese is the New Year's celebration, called *Ganjitsu*. Traditionally, Ganjitsu lasts several days. During that period, people visit friends' and relatives' homes to talk, eat, and exchange New Year's greetings. (*"Ake mashite omedeto!"*) They eat *ozoni* (rice cake dipped in soy sauce and sugar), *mame* (sugared black beans), *kazunoko* (herring roe), *konbu* (seaweed), *konnyaku* (yam noodle cake), *renkon* (lotus roots), *takenoko* (bamboo shoots), *kamaboko* (fish cakes), *ebi* (shrimp), *tai* (salt-water fish), *shiitake* (black mushrooms), and *mikan* (oranges) and drink *sake* (wine). Ganjitsu is a time for polite conversation and traditional Japanese games, such as *iroha karuta* (alphabet card game) and *uta karuta* (poetry card game).

The Japanese Boys' Festival is observed on May 5 each year. The boys bring out their lacquered armor and swords or fly a colorful cloth kite in the breeze. The kite is a symbol of virility and good fortune. The Nisei boys' interest in this festival and the New Year's festival has generally been lukewarm—sufficient to placate their parents.

Japanese culture has generally been more appealing to adult Nisei women. Some recollections of a Nisei woman follow:

> For most Nisei, the greatest single influence was their parents. Their character almost determined our lives. Lucky for us that they were, most of them, truly good people. By dominating us they rather insulated us from the outside influences, and perhaps that was just as well because most of us were raised in the poorest types of environments. The other night, after everyone was in bed, I sat by the window, listening to the rain and drinking tea. I remembered my mother.
>
> I was rather a timid, shy girl and greatly influenced by my mother. She was not a well-educated person but intelligent. She impressed me with the facts that I must get a good education and develop artistic interest. This was a little unusual because we were poor by American standards, and many Issei believed girls should be married off. Higher education was reserved for boys. My father, an honest, hard-working man, did not have too much influence on me, but he did not object to my mother's ideas about raising children, and he was extremely proud if we did well at school.
>
> Like most of my friends, I was given the opportunity to learn about the Japanese language, flower

Nisei girls perform a cherry blossom dance for a young people's entertainment.

arrangement, and *odori*. Most of us went through these lessons mechanically. After the public school hours were over, we would stop at a grocery for candy and then arrive just in time for class. Those poor dedicated teachers! They did their best but it wasn't enough. Very little Japanese sank into our heads though we attended year after year....

Every day after Japanese class, I would walk to my odori class with my sister and a few friends. We bought lesson tickets for the sum of twenty-five cents each, quite a sacrifice for my parents. In the winter time, it would be dark by the time we finished our *odori* lessons. Since the meaning of Japanese dancing is in the accompanying song, its true beauty escaped me entirely till I discovered Japanese literature in my later years. Of course, it was fun to play with our friends while we waited our turns.

We did develop grace and a great feeling of respect for our teacher. Her word was law and no pupil, adult or child, ever questioned her authority. We bowed to her before each lesson. She taught *odori, shamisen* (lute), voice and drum. Her whole repertoire was classified in her head, pounded into her since she was three....

There were some traditions and beliefs that my mother observed in her everyday life that affected me in a more subtle way. Any auspicious occasion as well as the first day of every month was celebrated with red rice, a mixture of sweet rice and red beans. Salt was used to ward off evil spirits....

We enjoyed Girls' Day. Every home with daughters celebrated the occasion by displaying their special dolls. The confectionery shops always had special *mochi* wrapped in cherry blossom leaves. To this day I buy the *sakura mochi* on March 3. I inherited my mother's superstitious fervor in the belief that this day must be observed to bring a felicitous fulfillment to my daughters' lives—a good happy marriage.

So much of my mother's life was bound by religious traditions. She had a Shinto shrine display where she prayed every day. She filled the water vessel with fresh water every morning. At night, the first scoop of hot rice was also offered at her little shrine. Every first fruit or vegetable of the season, and special food gifts from friends, were first placed in her shrine. I gathered that the objects of worship pervaded the entire life around her.

When anyone in the family started a new project she would pray, even when she started to cut material for a new dress. When we bought a new piece of furniture or tea kettle, she prayed. When she saw the new moon, she always prayed, adding, "How could

it be so beautiful?'' thus enhancing its beauty for me
for the rest of my life.

I think that her prayers sustained her lonely life in
a foreign country. It was as if she were praying to
everything in her environment, so that it would be
friendly to her, good to her.

As a little girl I remember the baths every night
and if she had time, she would tell us Japanese fairy
tales. In the summer time as we snuggled between
the cold sheets, the room would still be dimly lit.

A woman playing the koto, a thirteen-string Japanese musical instrument.

When she washed my hair, I remember her comb-
ing it and saying that beautiful black hair was a
woman's treasure. She reminisced that just before
she boarded the boat for America she walked into a
little comb shop in Yokohama. A gray-haired
woman waited on her and admired my mother's
heavy black hair. She gave her a tortoise comb for
good luck in the new country.

The Japanese art of flower arrangement, *ikebana,* means
living flower. A Nisei student of this art explains it as showing
"the awareness of nature or oneness with nature." Although
there are many schools of flower arrangement in Japan and in
the United States, "all of them stress heaven, earth, and
man—man's relation to the universe." It is an ancient art,
originating as long ago as the sixth or seventh century. Buddhist
monks finding flowers and branches along the road would put
them in vases and place them before the image in the sanctuary.

Japanese gardening and the tea ceremonies came to Japan
with Zen monks from China. Japanese ideals as well as the
physical situation in Japan—namely, its small size—are demonstrated in the gardening, which capitalizes on the beauty of
the smallest object. Unlike the often lavish Western concept of
beauty, the Japanese have used their extraordinary discipline to
create beauty in even the smallest areas. The art of *bonsai,*
meaning "'dwarf tree" or "'potted dwarf tree,'" has been passed
on from generation to generation in Japan. The potted land-
scapes offer a hint of a piece of scenery and are aimed at an
aesthetic effect. Again, the intent is not to overwhelm the
spectator, as so often occurs in Western art.

The enjoyment derived from Japanese gardening arises from
nature's potential and variation. Flowers may be removed during pruning since the shape and foliage of the shrub is the
important thing. Evergreen plantings are common, and decidu-
ous trees and shrubs are utilized so that their winter beauty is
apparent. A Japanese American landscape gardener sum-
marizes the underlying principles of garden planning in this

An example of ikebana, the Japanese art of flower arrangement, from the Ikenobo School.

This replica of a 500-year-old garden in Kyoto, Japan, has been created in the Brooklyn Botanic Garden in New York.

The Roji Garden at the Brooklyn Botanic Garden is an example of the traditional use of stone, plants, and water to create a harmonious setting.

An example of the art of bonsai, the creation of a potted dwarf tree.

way. "The traditional Japanese garden is designed and constructed according to rigid aesthetic principles. Every element has its place. Every object from ground cover to bridge has a purpose, even if it is only symbolical."

The traditional garden in America is usually fairly large, and is intended for public enjoyment. The Japanese family garden, on the other hand, is usually a small intimate area hidden behind walls or fences. It is designed for living rather than display and is seldom seen by anyone other than the immediate family and guests. Most family gardens of Japanese Americans are somewhat freer in their expression than traditional Japanese gardens. They show more individual expression in their treatment of the three traditional elements in a Japanese garden: stone, the natural framework; plants, which bring life to the garden; and water, which sets the mood.

Judo has long been a part of Japanese culture. The word *judo* means "the gentle way," and that is how most Japanese with basic judo skill have handled the sport. In this century, judo has become popular in non-Japanese society. World War II added to judo's stature. About 1942, the U.S. military began to take a keen interest in judo. At the Judo Institute in Chicago, Masato Tamura, a black belt judo expert, proved to a select group of navy and marine corps officers the value of judo in combat fighting. Tamura met 205-pound Karl Pojello, a Lithuanian-born professional wrestler, who was positive that he could make any judo expert surrender by using wrestling tactics. Tamura defeated Pojello in one minute and ten seconds. The *Chicago Times* sports editor was so impressed by this fantastic feat that he devoted a whole column to the exhibition.

Two participants demonstrate their skill at the sport of judo, the "gentle way."

Before World War II, interest in Japanese flower arrangement, gardening, judo, and the tea ceremony was limited to the more sophisticated among the Issei and Nisei. After World War II, it extended into the non-Japanese society.

It is not easy to estimate the impact of Japanese culture on the Sansei, whose parents, the Nisei, are drifting somewhat away from Japanese ways. Some observers see in the Sansei a certain resistance to their cultural heritage. The Sansei feel themselves to be much more American than Japanese. They want to have a say in their positions as Americans and to have some effect on American values. Prejudicial activities by other Americans, such as discriminatory hiring practices, are causing them to speak out about their role as Japanese Americans. The Sansei feel the Japanese have given much too much for the United States to cast them aside.

Still, many Sansei are conscious of Japanese culture, and study the Japanese customs, history, and language. And they are applying Japanese norms to American situations, taking after their Issei grandparents in their ways of dealing with their own particular affairs. Looking at the whole group of Sansei, it seems assured that some forms of Japanese culture will continue.

9.
What They Do for a Living

A Japanese immigrant who was dispatched by an employment agency to a white household chuckled over his first encounter with the strange English language. The employer barked out an order, handed him a broom and a dust pan, and then pointed a finger at the floor in the room. The Japanese didn't understand a word said but it was obvious the man wanted the room cleaned. After he struggled through a day's work, the Japanese was rewarded with a silver dollar. To the Japanese, it was a fortune, and he was grateful. After all, the only English words he understood then were *yes* and *no*.

Take the case of the Japanese who worked in a drugstore. A fellow rushed into his place and shouted, "Hurry up, delivery." But for the life of him, the Japanese couldn't find any "hurry up" among the things stocked in the store. How was he to know what "hurry up" meant or that he was to give the man an item for delivery in a hurry?

Despite the obvious language barrier, the Japanese have survived in this country and have succeeded, as individuals and as a group, in improving their situation here.

The first Japanese to arrive in America came not merely in search of great sums of money. They were not ignorant, narrowly ambitious laborers seeking higher wages. The early Japanese immigrants were mostly students who, filled with the idea of progress, came to the United States to study and learn. While they often worked as servants, this was only a means of getting an education. The "school boys," as they came to be known, provided an example of Japanese ambition and desire to progress. While the agricultural laborers who came later were not as well educated as the early immigrants, they were not content to remain laborers and quickly worked their way up to become tenant farmers and independent farmers. The Japanese have shown themselves to be too ambitious to remain at one position when there are better opportunities elsewhere.

The success of the Japanese in agriculture has been mentioned in earlier chapters. During the period before the alien land laws were enacted, the Japanese immigrants received an in-depth course in farming. They quickly learned new ways of producing and distributing goods and services. By specializing in high-profit crops, the Japanese were able to buy more and more land for farming. Their achievements in turning California's soil into a fruitful crop-bearing land and in developing rock gardening are part of California's history.

The first Japanese settlers in San Joaquin County planted grapes in the Acampo area shortly after their arrival in 1885. Today, their descendants control one-third of Lodi's famous Flame Tokay grapes. Early Japanese settlers in the Santa Cruz Mountains also cultivated grapes as well as plums and other crops. Cotton production in California was pioneered in 1909 by the Japanese who turned the first spades of soil in the rich Imperial Valley.

With the introduction of railroad lines into the Northwest in the late nineteenth century, the Japanese began to take up dairy farming and soon were responsible for half the milk supply in the large cities of the Northwest. From there, they went to market gardening and berry growing. In 1923, about 70 percent of Japanese produce in the Northwest was marketed to supply demands of many eastern cities.

A Japanese farmer described Seattle's Japanese farming community of pre-World War II days this way:

> All truck gardening was a family enterprise. Women and children would sit around the table, tying up

bundles of vegetables. They joked, kidded, talked, sang, and devised other schemes to while away the time. This may go on till past bedtime as the occasion demands....

Vegetables were shipped by horse and wagon to wholesale commission houses on Western Avenue, to Pike Place Market, and to scattered outlets such as Pacific Fruit & Produce Co. Some of the vegetables were transacted in direct sales at Sixth Avenue and Dearborn Street where the farmers met the throng of thriving independent Japanese grocers.

One of the hazards of farmers in their daily journey was traveling through Georgetown which had a reputation for being tough even on whites. Many of the Issei saw fit to carry side-arms for protection.

Alien land laws enacted in the western states reduced the number of Japanese farmers working there. Legislators in the state of Washington, for example, took aim at the Japanese farmers by prohibiting every interest in land, and any "right to the control, possession, use, enjoyment, rents, issues or profits thereof." This act was passed in 1921. In 1923 a second act made it a violation of the first alien land law if non-declarant aliens were found upon land owned, rented, or otherwise held by their minor children citizens. This second law meant that parents were forbidden to act as guardians for the real property of their minor children, though the latter were secure in their right to own, buy, sell, rent, lease, or otherwise obtain and hold interest in farm land.

The anti-alien land laws were repealed after World War II—too late to benefit the Issei who by then were too old to continue farming. Today, the number of Japanese employed in agriculture is greatly reduced, largely because the Sansei are not interested in farming as a career and are moving to the cities.

During the late nineteenth and early twentieth centuries, Japanese labored on railroads and in sawmills and canneries. In general, they achieved satisfactory relations with their employers because of their efficiency. On the railroads, in particular, Japanese succeeded in getting better wages than other minority groups and became very popular workers with the employers. The large number of Japanese employed by the railroads in the early part of this century is largely due to the number of Japanese contractors, who secured laborers for the railroads.

Japanese working in lumber mills in the early twentieth century were unable to receive wages equal to those paid white workers. In 1907, about 30 percent (2,685) of the Japanese adult males in Washington were employed in logging and lumber camps. By 1924, the number had dropped to 1,458, a decrease of 46 percent since 1907, despite the fact that the total number of employees in the industry had increased 30 percent during this period.

The "Little Tokyos" which sprang up mainly on the West Coast provided an opportunity for Japanese to open businesses catering to other Japanese. As the populations of these communities grew, they began to establish vital businesses such as grocery stores, restaurants, hotels, and barber shops. As early

The business center of the Japanese section of Los Angeles in 1912.

as 1909, Portland's Japanese barbers were organized with their own union. They charged twenty-five cents for a haircut and ten cents for a shave, the same prices charged by the majority of Caucasian-owned barber shops in that city. Outside the communities, Japanese businesses met with hostility and usually did not succeed. Also, jobs suitable to their education and skills were often denied to the Japanese. College graduates working as clerks in grocery stores and on produce rows were not uncommon. Indeed, some Japanese were forced to return to Japan.

The problems faced by one West Coast Nisei man illustrate some of the difficulties of the educated Japanese. Noboru Nishisaka graduated from a university as a Phi Beta Kappa, *magna cum laude*, and with a degree in electrical engineering. Yet, when electrical engineering firms sent their representatives to the campus to interview top students, his professor advised him that since he wouldn't be hired anyway, he should look for work elsewhere. Discouraged, Nishisaka left the United States, for the only "elsewhere" he could think of was Japan. Finding a job in Japan wasn't easy for Nishisaka because he had only a nodding acquaintance with the Japanese language, but after a time, he learned. Today, he is doing well and is involved in a joint venture with an American firm.

Many Nisei women were hired as clerks and secretaries, although, as one Japanese American woman recalls,

Before World War II, teachers tried to discourage [us] from taking secretarial courses. But we went ahead and studied, anyway, for a secretarial career. After graduation, we started looking for jobs. Jobs, in those days, were hard to come by. Sheer determination kept us trying. We were hired, retained, and in time advanced into positions of responsibility and trust, on merit alone.

One woman who aspired to be a registered nurse in 1928 caused quite a stir in her hometown. An irate American wrote to a newspaper: "Why, if I was in a hospital, I wouldn't let that creature touch me.'' Eventually, the Nisei was admitted to training and graduated with honors.

It was not until after World War II that the door to job opportunities was swung wide open to all Japanese Americans. The remainder of this chapter will be devoted to individuals who overcame the hardships and succeeded in America both before and after World War II.

The attitude of the Japanese toward success and their determination to succeed are reflected in the story of Masuo Yasui, who became the most influential Japanese in the Oregon agricultural region of Hood River. Yasui had been reared in Japan. After graduating from high school, he came to the United States in 1901 at the age of sixteen to join his older brothers.

Yasui first found work on the railroad, and then accepted a job as a houseboy for an attorney. For his services he was given a small salary with his room and board, but the biggest compensation was that his employer gave him access to his law library and discussed various law cases with him. Reading law books and carrying on discussions with the attorney, coupled with some formal training at night, allowed young Yasui to become proficient in English. Soon after, he decided to settle on his own in Hood River, Oregon.

One of Yasui's sons recalls his father's story this way:

> A small Japanese combination boarding house-store existed in Hood River at this time, which catered to the young Japanese who worked on the railroad and sawmills in the vicinity. In 1908, my father with his older brother, Renichi, came to Hood River, and with their meager savings pooled together, bought the boarding house-store operation. Being inexperienced in business, short of capital, and supported only by a small clientele, my father and his brother were barely able to keep up their business. So, in order to pump new money into the embryonic partnership, my father went to work as a janitor in the town bank to support the store. Not wishing to tar-

nish his newly acquired reputation as a businessman, Dad worked his janitorial shift during the early morning hours so he would be seen toiling by a minimum of people.

As a youngster and during my growing years, I can remember my father constantly encouraging us to do our best in whatever venture we undertook. He reminded us constantly that since we were of a minority race, we would have to excel to even be given the chance to compete with fellow Americans. He kept reminding us that we were Americans and that as such we should become good Americans. His concern for us was that we would accept our citizenship complacently and that all the God-given benefits of citizenship would be expected by us, rather than earned. Still, he told us to always be proud of our Japanese heritage. Had citizenship been available for alien Japanese at this time, I am certain my father would have been one of the first to apply.

Being in business in Hood River and for many years the only Japanese family living in the city, Yasui's American friends were primarily professional and business people. Though the Alien Land Law existed during this period, Yasui encouraged the Japanese in the growing community to save their money and to purchase land. He assisted them in establishing guardianships and trusts for the minor children through the help of understanding Caucasian friends. Since the Nisei in the 1920s and 1930s were not of legal age, possibly as much as 75 percent of the Japanese-occupied farms were held in trust or guardianship. That the Japanese now living in Hood River are enjoying the fruits of their labor is, in large measure, a tribute to Yasui's foresight. One Hood River man recalls, "He was almost stubborn in his determination to uphold his principles and beliefs."

Not all Japanese immigrants had as difficult a struggle as the Yasui family. The Saibaras emigrated from Japan in 1903 and brought ten thousand dollars in cash and several rice-growing specialists with them. They bought land in Texas and have grown rice there for over sixty years.

In 1909, Yoichi Agari, Yurikuma Imachi, and Saikichi Yamada introduced the chrysanthemum floriculture into San Mateo, California. This is one of the industries still carried on almost exclusively by Japanese Americans.

Japanese oysters were brought and introduced to America by Emy Tsukimoto and Joe Miyagi, who first tested them in a bay off the state of Washington. Their success helped bolster the oyster industry in that state.

One Issei who is particularly well remembered is Tokinosuke Sekine, who was Jack London's houseboy at that author's Glen Ellen, California, ranch.

"It was my job to wake him up in the mornings so he could write," Sekine recalled. When London died, Sekine prepared the "eternal bed" in the custom of his country. The bedroom was tidied up, a single red flower was placed on the pillow, and into the breast pocket was inserted this note: "Your speech was silver, your silence is now golden." As long as Sekine was at the ranch, a fresh red flower was laid on London's pillow. Visitors still note a single red flower propped on pillow at the home, perpetuating a tribute begun by Sekine.

Of course, all the Japanese immigrants to the mainland United States did not arrive or remain in the West Coast states. Many Japanese who settled along the East Coast and inland encountered problems similar to those of their West Coast counterparts. They did not speak, read, or write English, and they knew nothing about American culture and folkways. These Japanese also met hostility and prejudice, although not on the same scale as on the West Coast where there were organized anti-Japanese movements. But despite these obstacles, they plunged ahead to a new way of life by competing for jobs with European immigrants, eking out a living, and saving money. There were those like Ryoichiro Arai, Oriye Kai, Toyo Morimura, Yasukata Murai, and Momotaro Sato who set their sights on international trade and commerce, and who figured in the establishment of Japanese companies in New York and later elsewhere throughout the United States. They were the pioneers who, through personal contacts, tact, patience, and integrity, gradually broke down certain stereotypes of Japanese commercial irresponsibility and dishonesty.

Among the more prominent Issei working on the East Coast was Dr. Jokichi Takamine, a distinguished scientist who introduced synthetic fertilizer to Japan. Dr. Takamine's greatest honor came after he isolated adrenaline as part of a project he was working on while employed as consultant for Parke Davis Company, New York.

A Japanese architect of considerable renown in the early 1900s was Yosuke W. Nakano. Recognized as an expert in the use of reinforced concrete, Nakano participated in the construction of more than two hundred major buildings on the East Coast, including fifty major buildings in Philadelphia, Pennsylvania.

Much of the credit for the landscaping in Miami Beach, Florida, is given to Kotaro Suto, a Japanese gardener who, on his own time, helped beautify the city with his landscape skills. Suto's contribution to the city was formally recognized in 1953 when he and his wife decided to leave for Japan. Suto did return to live out his remaining years in the city he had helped build and had come to love.

Another Issei who left his mark was Hachiro Onuki, who was instrumental in the introduction of the first street lights in 1886 in Phoenix, Arizona. This was made possible when he and two associates were granted a franchise by Phoenix to supply that city with lighting.

The man who was to contribute most significantly to Chicago's Japanese community arrived in 1916 after a successful business venture at the St. Louis Fair. He was Yasuma Yamasaki, who was the originator of the Dime restaurants which were patronized by many grateful people during the Great Depression.

Turning now from the successes of the first-generation

Japanese, we should take a look at the contributions of the Nisei, who have also had to surmount tremendous obstacles in order to succeed in America.

America has had many Japanese Americans in politics. Senator Daniel Inouye, Representative Spark Matsunaga, and Representative Patsy (Takemoto) Mink are three outstanding legislators from Hawaii. Inouye was seriously considered as a vice-presidential candidate in 1968 at the Democratic National Convention in Chicago at which he was the keynote speaker. Another Nisei political figure from Hawaii is George Ariyoshi, who was elected governor in 1974.

The first Nisei to be elected to a state-level position on the mainland was Seiji Horiuchi of Brighton, Colorado. Mr. Horiuchi served one term in the Colorado State Legislature. Three Nisei in California, including Norman Mineta of San Jose, have become mayors of their cities; the first was elected in 1966.

The Nisei have also been successful in the arts and sciences and have made names for themselves in many other fields.

Bob Okazaki, an actor and probably the most knowledgeable person alive when it comes to reciting the triumphs of Japanese performers, remembers many Japanese in show business before World War II. There were the Tanaka sisters from Los Angeles dancing on a Mississippi River showboat; Sojin Kamiyama acting as one of the Three Wise Men for Cecil B. deMille and later starring as the first Chinese detective in the Charlie Chan series; Sessue Hayakawa, the best known of them all; Arthur Kaihatsu, who acted in Hal Roach's "Our Gang" comedies and who was also briefly a member of Mickey McGuire's moppets; Hizi Koyke, who became known on Broadway for her operatic role in *Madame Butterfly,* and Tsuru Aoki, the first woman of Japanese ancestry to star in Hollywood films, who later became Hayakawa's wife through the intervention of a baishakunin.

While these performers shared the world of Hollywood with other film giants, Japanese in other communities set up their own more modest, small-scale world of klieg lights and greasepaint. Before Pearl Harbor, small theaters were scattered up and down the West Coast, where the bulk of the mainland Japanese population was concentrated.

Shortly after World War II ended, Hollywood suddenly ''re-discovered'' the Japanese. While films prior to the war often treated the Japanese unfairly and according to common stereotypes, films depicting the Japanese in a more favorable light began to appear after World War II. More Japanese were featured in the films. Such tried, experienced cinema veterans as Sessue Hayakawa, Teru Shimada and Bob Okazaki returned to the screen. Newcomers included James Shigeta, Jack Soo (Suzuki), George Takei, Nobu McCarthy, Miiko Taka, Miiko Mayama and Michi Kobi.

Takei, a veteran of movies and television, commented on the Japanese situation in Hollywood as it had changed in the years of film-making. Speaking of the appearance of Japanese in pre-World War II films, Takei said:

> The depiction of Asians was singularly stereotyped; they were one-dimensional caricatures. The temper of the times lent itself to this sort of characterization I suppose and the absence of true actors contributed to it. Anybody available would rush out to the studios to answer a call. They were cast, not for any acting ability, but for the flavor they brought to the script. They were simply selling their Asian appearances. Thus, they were not working to bring any semblance of truth to their performances but merely to accommodate the preconceived and almost always stereotyped notions of the white directors. It is this legacy that we are saddled with today and this is what we must work to change.
>
> I think the depiction today isn't as blatantly and as obviously negative as it was then but there are still subtle and sometimes very profoundly affecting ramifications to the portrayals of Asians on films and television.

Actor George Takei in a scene from television's "Star Trek."

The perspective is still from the white vantage point so that the Asian characters are seen through a scrim of exotica. The emphasis is on the foreignness rather than on the humanity of the character.

Opportunities to portray Asian American characters are extremely rare. And here I feel the media is really remiss in fully reflecting the rich, pluralistic fabric of American society. When those opportunities do occur, one senses a heavy-handed delineation of the ''Americanness'' of the character—the overly hip dialogue, the exaggeratedly Western attitudes and usually the complete alienation from the Asian heritage. The character becomes an Asian-faced ''American'' stereotype.

Our community [Los Angeles] is becoming very aware of this and to the importance of exerting some influence in bringing about changes.

The black movement has really been at the spearhead of this effort. It has articulated the issue—the power of the media to perpetuate negative images as well as its capacity of renovating those pictures. It has opened the minds of the powers-that-be and sensitized them to the importance of detailed, humanized, truthful portrayals of minority groups. We can be the beneficiaries of their pioneering. But from here on, we must do our own work ourselves.

This means we must start to produce our own writers—artists who can provide us with the keenly personal observation, that finely sensed detail, that nuance that defines what it means to be Asian American. We must produce our directors who can breathe life into these writings. We are developing our performing artists who give voice and body to these creations. And most of all, we've got to develop audiences that will bring ultimate fulfillment

to these works. We've only begun this effort. We
have a long way to go.

In the field of letters, one of the best-known Japanese Americans is S. I. Hayakawa, semanticist, jazz historian, author, and
former college president. He is the author of the popular
Language in Action, and he emerged as a national figure when
he restored order at student-troubled San Francisco State College. Gospel singer Mahalia Jackson once said, ''He was a
pioneer in inter-racial relations back in Chicago when it was not
fashionable to be so.''

Around the early 1900s, there was a substantial following
among Japanese in America of Joaquin Miller, the poet of the
Sierras. The late Japanese American newspaperman Tamotsu
Murayama described some of the bohemians and poets who
became disciples of Miller. ''They represent the original cultural movement of the Japanese in America. Japan's noted poet
Yonejiro Noguchi stands out among Miller's students. Then
only 20 years old, Noguchi became a student of Miller in the fall
of 1893, staying with him for ten years before going to the East
Coast. Other Japanese bohemians who followed Miller were
'Prince' Kanae Nagasawa and Isen Kanno.''[21]

Taro Yashima, an artist-author from Los Angeles, was a
grand prix winner in the Twenty-third International Art Show
held in the fall of 1972 in Paris. President Lyndon B. Johnson's
chief photographer was Yoichi Robert Okamoto, who is said to
have taken as many as 250,000 pictures of the President while
he was in office. Genichiro Nishio, painter-photographer in
Washington, D.C., made a name for himself for his portraits of
top public figures, including every President since Woodrow
Wilson.

Minoru Yamasaki is a world renowned architect whose works
include the IBM (International Business Machines) building in
Seattle, the World Trade Center in New York, and the Science
Pavilion at the Seattle Center.

The Dallas-Fort Worth Regional Airport in Texas was designed by Nisei architect Gyo Obata of St. Louis, Missouri.

The Northwestern National Life Insurance Company building
(above) in Minneapolis, Minnesota, and the $10 million U.S.
Science Pavilion for Seattle's Century I Exposition in 1962.
Both buildings were designed by architect Minoru Yamasaki.

Then there are photographers like the late Toge Fujihira of New York and Henry Ushijima of Chicago; artist Mine Okubo, who gained fame with ''Citizen 13660,'' a series of black and white illustrations of life during evacuation and incarceration of Japanese Americans; interior furnishings creator George Nakashima; and painter Henry Sugimoto.

Dr. Makio Murayama, research biochemist at the National Institutes of Health, Bethesda, Maryland, discovered the cause of and later a way to treat sickle-cell anemia. He built and studied a three-foot-high model of a molecule magnified 127 million times. Dr. Paul Terasaki, professor of surgery at the University of California at Los Angeles, developed a tissue compatibility test which played a prominent role in the first heart transplant operations.

In the sports world, organized baseball attracted Japanese, and there was no color bar. In the early 1900s, several Japanese players in the Pacific Northwest were good enough to receive offers to play professional ball. Two Japanese Americans who made the minor leagues were Jimmy Horio, an outfielder, and Ken Nushida, a pitcher. Both played in the Pacific Coast League. Probably the first Japanese American to umpire in a non-Japanese league was Kay Takayoshi of the City League in Seattle. Hank Matsubu, a catcher from Portland, Oregon, was signed up by the Pittsburgh Pirates.

Just as the whites did not discriminate against the Japanese Americans in baseball, the Nisei had no bars against non-Japanese playing in their leagues. Fred Haney, once a major league baseball star, was on the roster for the first Japanese American baseball club, which was organized in 1914 in Los Angeles.

Two big-time college football players were Joe Nagata and Jim Kishi, both of whom saw action in major college football bowl games in January 1944. Nagata, a first-string quarterback for the Louisiana State University Tigers, was an outstanding player when LSU defeated Texas A & M in the annual Orange Bowl game on New Year's Day in 1944. At the Cotton Bowl,

Kishi, a tackle, played for the University of Texas Longhorns as they tied the Randolph Field Fliers.

Perhaps the most outstanding Nisei college football player in the post-World War II years was Pete Domoto. Domoto was guard and co-captain of the University of California's Golden Bears, who played in the Rose Bowl game of 1959.

Wally Yonamine from Hawaii played for the San Francisco Forty-Niners during the 1949-1950 football season. He is believed to be the only Nisei ever to have played major professional football in the United States. After a season as understudy to the great Frankie Alberts, Yonamine turned to professional baseball and played for the Salt Lake Bees in the Pioneer League. He later joined the Tokyo Giants in Japan's Central League.

Two Nisei basketball players made their marks in major college competition. They were Ted Ohashi, of the University of California Bears, and Wat Misaka, of the University of Utah. Ohashi, a West Coast all-star selection, was the first Nisei ever to star on a college basketball team on the U.S. mainland, and he was a hero to the Japanese sports fans in the early thirties. Ohashi recalls an incident that occurred during his college basketball days. He remembers one player whom he played against during his freshman year at the University of California. After a particularly tough game, Ohashi says: "The fellow sought me out and said, 'I want to apologize to you for my conduct. You see, I never had any contact with a Japanese before.' He was big enough to regret his rough play and I appreciated his coming over to talk to me."

Like Ohashi, Misaka was a guard. He was top reserve on the University of Utah team which in 1944 won the national collegiate championship and starting guard on the quintet which in 1946 captured the National Invitational Tournament title. When the National Basketball Association opened its 1947-48 season, Misaka was signed on by the New York Knicks. The Nisei's stay in pro ball was brief. Misaka, after all, was only five foot seven.

Bill Kajikawa, a 1937 Arizona State University graduate, who has been inducted into the Arizona Basketball Hall of Fame, was head basketball coach of the Arizona State team from 1948 to 1957.

In the Olympic Games of 1952, Ford Konno and Yoshi Oyakawa, both of Hawaii, won gold medals in swimming. Later, in the 1956 and 1960 Olympics, Tommy Kono of Sacramento earned gold medals in weightlifting.

A third-generation Japanese American has gained national honors in tennis. She is Ann Kiyomura of San Mateo, California. In 1966, she won the U.S. girls' twelve-and-under singles title at Chattanooga, Tennessee. Then on August 12, 1972, at Philadelphia, she won the U.S. girls' eighteen-and-under singles crown.

The aim of this chapter has been to give some idea of the improvements which Japanese Americans made in their condition since their arrival and since the critical years of the evacuation, the internment camps, and World War II. By surviving the humiliating experience of mass evacuation during World War II, when the Nisei and their parents were stripped of all that was dear to them, the Japanese Americans emerged as a more mature group determined to prove themselves worthy of a respectable place in the American scheme of things.

10.
The Nonconformists

The Japanese, on the whole, have liked the image of the good citizen, for this has been an aid in their reaching certain rungs on the social and economic ladders. In order to adapt to, and live comfortably in, the United States, the Japanese have had to conform to American standards. While most Japanese have been guided by the needs of the group, there were, and are, dissidents who set out to assert their individuality. This chapter will take a look at this minority of the disenchanted, who have met life in the United States differently from the main group of Japanese.

During the first wave of Japanese immigration in the nineteenth century, a concern of the Japanese government was the possible negative effects of the *shosei* (pseudo students) in San Francisco on the American image of the Japanese in general. In an informal census taken in 1888 the San Francisco Japanese consul had estimated that from 70 to 80 percent of the 2,000 Japanese in the city and its fringes referred to themselves as *shosei*, all of whom, the consul sadly observed, were young, unemployed, and on the verge of starvation. The disturbing report did not set well with the Japanese government. Munemitsu Mutsu, a newly-appointed resident minister to the United States, was ordered to stop over in San Francisco en route to Washington, D.C., to personally inquire into the matter. To his surprise, Mutsu learned that jobs were available even to the most ignorant and indolent among the shosei. He found that they could exist by merely working a few days since there were numerous Japanese community organizations which provided shelter and simple Japanese food for twenty to thirty cents a day. Mutsu's dispatch back to Japan recommended that the shosei be classed as *dekaseginin* (birds of passage) rather than *imin* (immigrant). The Japanese government could offer this distinction as an explanation if public attention were focused on the shosei as a rationale for opposition to the presence of the Japanese in the United States.

Mutsu's report on San Francisco's shosei stimulated Japan's interest in the Japanese in America. As one of several investigation attempts, Yoshiro Fujita, the secretary of the consulate in San Francisco, was delegated to inquire about the Japanese in Washington and Oregon. He discovered a highly irregular situation in Seattle. Many of the immigrants living there were on the shady side of the law. An effort to expel the undesirables by cooperating with American authorities was suggested at a community meeting but nothing happened. Fujita reported that those attending the meeting were "all apprehensive . . . and feared that the gamblers and their associates would try everything to ruin their business if the latter learned of the former's attempt. And, some even thought that their lives might be threatened."

Attempts by the Seattle Japanese to police themselves proved futile, so Fujita next appealed to the chief of police to suppress both gambling and prostitution to protect the reputation of respectable Japanese. The chief flatly refused. Puzzled, Fujita demanded an explanation, and the chief replied that "not only Japanese but Irish, Swedes and other nationalities had been engaged in prostitution...and [therefore] it was impossible for them [the police] to punish only the Japanese." Fujita was flabbergasted at this unusual statement of equal treatment, but he later heard that the police chief had been bribed to ignore the vice rackets.[22]

Other nonconforming Japanese Americans broke away from conventional society in different ways. Artists and writers sometimes joined other Americans in assuming the bohemian lifestyle.

Perhaps the most flamboyant of all American bohemians was Sadakichi Hartmann (1867-1944), a naturalized citizen of Japanese-German ancestry. A description of Hartmann was presented in the *San Francisco Chronicle*:

> Who could be more modern than the long-haired Sadakichi Hartmann in a Prince Albert jacket who struck an insouciant pre-Raphaelite pose while standing on a pedestal six feet high in a 1896 photograph? Who more modern than the man who wrote the first script for a psychedelic light show in 1895, composed haiku as early as 1898, and was banned in Boston in 1893 and jailed for a drama that rivaled *Oh, Calcutta* in nude scenes? Who more modern than Hartmann who studied life in communes, wrote some of the earliest film criticism in 1912, advocated sexual freedom and women's liberation, and argued the coming revolution with Emma Goldman and her lover, Alexander Berkman?[23]

The great and near great in American art and literature knew of Hartmann; some adored him, and others despised him. Walt Whitman, for instance, said in 1888 that he had "more hope, more faith" in Hartmann than "any of the boys." James Gibbons Huneker said that Hartmann literally "exudes genius." In contrast, Sheridan Ford denounced Hartmann as "the most dangerous man in the world" after reading his erotic poetry. Ben Hecht brushed Hartmann off as a "truculent poseur" while W.C. Fields called him a "no-good drunken bum." Ezra Pound, however, said that if he had not been himself, he would have liked to have been Hartmann. While speaking nostalgically in his *Minutes of the Last Meeting* about the days of such as John Barrymore and W.C. Fields, Gene Fowler sketched Hartmann as an alcoholic moocher non-pareil and a "magnificent charlatan."[24] Hartmann spent his last years in poverty—posing as an "Indian" to escape internment during World

War II—and newspapers referred to him as America's last bohemian when he died in 1944.

During the jazz age in the twenties, the most outstanding group of Japanese dissidents was the *yogores* (the dirty ones). These were young people who dressed in dirtier-the-better yellow corduroy pants, a silk shirt, a saucer-like pancake hat or cap, and a crewneck sweater. Their hangouts were cafes, pool halls, speakeasies, theaters, taxi-dance halls, and, naturally, the gambling houses.

The yogores (pronounced yoh-go-rehs) made pocket money by working in fish canneries, the public market, sawmills, and restaurants. Some sold bonds, insurance policies, and securities; others worked on the farms.

A feeling of camaraderie was strong among the yogores. They followed the motto, "What's mine is yours and what's yours is mine." They observed their own rules of conduct and respected the law. For instance, if anyone in the gang became obnoxious at a speakeasy or wherever he happened to be, the others tied up the misbehaving youth and carted him home. Plucking apples off a homeowner's tree was the extent of their crime wave against society. Generally speaking, they were not violent people, and in the world in which they somehow managed to survive, the yogores remained silent.

The depression of the 1930s brought onto the American scene the *furyo seinen* (bad youths). The furyo seinen (pronounced fu-ryo say-nen) were the Japanese zoot suiters, and they were easy to spot. They wore dark pin-striped suits and bell-bottomed pants. Their hair style was the ducktail, slick and neatly combed. The furyo seinen considered themselves to be real smoothies.

Like the yogores of the twenties, the furyo seinen gathered at the pool halls, gambling houses, dance halls, theaters, and cafes. Their problems were unemployment and having a shortage of money. Looking at them, one would have quickly concluded that they were shiftless, aimless, and purposeless. Nothing could be further from the truth, for they were always on the hustle, always on the make for quick dough.

The job discrimination facing many Japanese gave the furyo seinen a dim view of conventional means of improvement and conventional employment. Too often, Japanese with college degrees were building their muscles in manual jobs. "Educated fools," the furyo seinen sneered. So, they dreamed up some rather ingenious methods of making money. For instance, they knocked over pinball machines by drilling holes in them and running wires through the machines to control the play. They sometimes used their own cars as taxis to earn a few dollars.

Since their folks worked, most of the furyo seinen lived at home. Their plight was not one of desperation for want of food or shelter—they thought nothing of spending half their money on flashy clothes—but desperation for something to do. They spent their time sleeping during the day and stepping out at night. Some of the parents eventually sent their children to Japan with the hope that they would shape up under the strict Japanese discipline.

To hear some old-timers talk, the yogores and the furyo seinen were not members of the human race. That, of course, is sheer nonsense. The yogores and the furyo seinen just happened to like their night life while the rest of the community slept. Neither group resorted to violence or crime. But for every yogore and furyo seinen, there were scores of other Japanese Americans who studied hard and attained scholastic and professional honors in spite of the fact that they were living in an area where gambling and other vices were prevalent. Sociology professor Robert Larsen at Seattle University once remarked, "The Japanese are an exception to the rule." If anything set the yogores and the furyo seinen apart from the other Japanese Americans, it was the clothes they wore and the playstyle they enjoyed. But compared to the youths on the wild drug scene in the late 1960s and early 1970s, the yogores and the furyo seinen were nothing more than restless young people.

Not all Japanese Americans had the same thoughts on their position during World War II. There was a small minority whose voices were filled with anger against the government that singled out the Japanese for evacuation to American concentration camps. They were the dissident young who sat out World War II in prison or went to Japan on a prisoner exchange program.

These youths were called the "no-no" boys, for they were the ones who answered no to two questions put before all Japanese over seventeen years of age whether they were U.S. citizens or not. The two questions were included in a questionnaire entitled "Application for Leave Clearance," and they pertained to the willingness of the Japanese to support America. They were: "Are you willing to serve in the armed forces of the United States on combat duty, wherever ordered ?" and "Will you swear unqualified allegiance to the United States of America and faithfully defend the United States from any attack by foreign or domestic forces, and foreswear any form of allegiance or obedience to the Japanese emperor, or to any other foreign government, power, or organization ?"

Some young Japanese American civilians protested their removal to relocation centers. Gordon Hirabayashi, a University of Washington student, defied both the curfew and evacuation orders and went to prison. Minoru Yasui, of Hood River, Oregon, challenged the military curfew order and was also imprisoned.

Two cases eventually reached the Supreme Court. Fred Korematsu, a native of Oakland, California, resisted evacuation and was convicted of staying in an area from which the Japanese were excluded. Mitsuye Endo, of Sacramento, California, became the central figure in a test case involving the right of the government to detain loyal American citizens in relocation centers. In 1944, the majority of the Supreme Court upheld the legality of evacuation based solely upon race in the Korematsu case, but in the same year, it ruled unanimously in favor of Miss Endo. In other words, the Supreme Court ruled that the evacuation was legal, but that the detention of Japanese Americans in relocation centers was illegal. The Endo case led to the army revoking its orders to exclude Japanese Americans from the West Coast.

When the boys came marching home from World War II, those behind prison walls and those who had gone to wartime Japan also returned to their homes. The veterans rejoined a grateful Japanese community, for they had enabled the Japanese to return triumphantly to the American society. The dissidents, on the other hand, filtered back to the taunts of critics, many of whom were war veterans. From the beginning, the climate was uncomfortably gloomy for the "no-no" boys, who were only grudgingly allowed to participate in community activities. While they were tolerated, the "no-nos" were exposed to widespread contempt. Often, their parents shared their suffering, and many openly blamed themselves for their sons' plight: "If only we had not tried to enforce our will . . . ."

During the sixties and seventies, the third generation of Japanese in America, the Sansei, has emerged. These young people are knowledgeable, outspoken, and idealistic. They are asking probing questions about the Japanese position in America. They want to know about double standards and about discrimination, and they seem determined to cut themselves loose from the shackles of injustices and inequities suffered by their parents and grandparents.

The Sansei declare it is ridiculous for the Japanese to think they have it made in the United States. If, for example, Japan's automotive, marine, and electronic industries should vigorously and aggressively capture the consumer market, causing a decline in the United States firms and throwing thousands out of work, who is to say that the non-Japanese in America would not direct their anger against the mainland Japanese? They are fearful that such an event could be the catalyst behind another wave of anti-Japanese sentiment. The fear is real to the Sansei—as real as their American citizenship, and as real as their Japanese faces.

A Nisei active in San Francisco sees tremendous potential in the Sansei because "they're not running around and asking people to make decisions for them'' and because ''they aren't afraid to take a stand on controversial issues.'' An editor of a San Francisco paper offered these comments:

They're still young but they're gradually asserting themselves. Several now own businesses but the most significant development is their involvement in three groups: Kimochi, Inc., which offers a recreational program for the Issei; the Japanese Community Youth Council which holds craft classes, summer day camp, discussion groups; and the Japanese Community Services which provides to the Issei information on old age, social security, medical and other services vital to the livelihood of the Issei.

In Los Angeles, the Sansei have helped found the Pioneer Center where the Issei can assemble for socials and games. They have also managed to get the state to hire bilingual personnel to assist Issei in need of social services. This achievement is

At the Pioneer Center in Los Angeles, goh and shogi are very popular.

People looking for sea shells on an outing to White Point, San Pedro, one of many field trips sponsored by the Los Angeles Pioneer Center.

reportedly unprecedented in the United States. Another Los Angeles Sansei project is providing care for the sightless Issei in their area. These instances of concern for the elderly indicate that some Sansei may aspire to goals other than the usual prestige professions.

During the late sixties and early seventies, the drug problem has plagued the American society, and it has not missed the Japanese communities. Unlike their parents, the Sansei have tried to cope with the situation. In Los Angeles, one of the early groups entering the fight against drug abuse was the "Yellow Brotherhood." The group was formed in 1969 by young people who themselves were once on drugs. According to a Los Angeles consultant, "It was a 'one-to-one' counseling by people who knew what they were talking about. The brotherhood did well in making the drug addicts realize that drug abuse was not the path to take."

Ron Wakabayashi, a former JACL field services director, hints that racism in the schools may be partly to blame for the Sansei youngsters' use of drugs. He paints an ugly picture of racism in some Los Angeles schools:

Every Friday, it's "Get the Jap Day" where the other youngsters go out beating up the Japanese kids .... A young lady last night was telling us that on December 7th one of the teachers had her and the other Japanese kids stand up and did not allow them to sit during class because "they" bombed Pearl Harbor. Another girl in junior high school in the east side of town recently was hit by her teacher and was told "I don't like Japs" and "I run the class the way I want and I don't like Japs."

In a 1968 radio program, "White Racism in America,"[25] a Nisei woman feelingly described how racism affects those who are discriminated against.

To you who discriminate against children because of race, I dedicate this essay, with the hope that you might reconsider. Have you ever wondered what happens to people you discriminate against? My parents came from Japan and settled in Hawaii where I was born, the last of ten children. I was almost eleven years old when the Japanese attacked Pearl Harbor. Until then, life was quite uneventful. If you have ever been to Hawaii, you will understand when I compare being brought up there with being in a huge fruit basket. Daily, one is surrounded by brown faces, yellow, white and black faces—Japanese, Filipino, Hawaiian, Spanish, Puerto Rican, Swede, German, Chinese—name it and you see it.

At eighteen, upon graduation from high school, I attended a college of about four hundred (all Caucasians) in Indiana. Each morning as a I brushed my teeth, I was startled by my reflection in the mirror, for no one else looked like me. Five years later, I married and followed my husband to Japan in Uncle Sam's Army. Walking the streets of my parents' homeland, again I was startled—this time by the masses of Japanese faces. I just was not used to being among people of one color—even when that color was the same as mine.…

Now, going back to Pearl Harbor—how drastically things changed! Overnight I was a "yellow Jap"—even to my Chinese school mates! The situation worsened when the first Army divisions came from the mainland. We were allowed to skip classes with V-for-Victory signs, but the soldiers soon knew the "Japs" from the Chinese, and, of course, the difference between us and the other races was even clearer.

So, even as a kid, how I wished my hair was blonde, my skin white, my eyes wide and deep-set, my nose straight and tall. How I hated my parents for being Japanese—they could at least have been Chinese! But "can the leopard change his spots?"

How well I remember, after being taunted at school about being a "sneaky Jap" and reminded of the atrocities committed against the U.S. prisoners of war by the Japanese, I went home and called my own parents "Japs." (Somehow my hurt was not assuaged.) How well do I also remember my oldest brother saying, "Go look in the mirror and see if you're a 'haole' (Hawaiian for Caucasian)."

I was "fortunate" enough to have two brothers join the U.S. Army—one in the 442nd, one in the 100th (the most decorated units in the U.S. Army)—so we could hang a service flag with two stars in our window. And every day my alien Japanese mother prayed that her two American sons would return with their lives, if not their legs, arms, or eyes. Return they did—one with a Purple Heart and scarred physically and emotionally for life.

Some said, "You Japanese sure proved your loyalty!" I say to them, "Why did we have to *prove* our loyalty?" Were Swedes ever *required* to *prove* their loyalty? Or the Irish, French, the Danes—or even the Germans and Italians? Are we not all *Americans*? Is not this the uniqueness of the United States of America? Do you require each member of *your* family to *prove* themselves a member? Is it not enough that he was born a Smith or a Moran or a Berquist? Or even adopted into your family?

So what do you really do to the children you discriminate against? You make them hate their parents; you make them hate themselves; you make them want to change an impossible situation. Therefore, you drive them to various forms of insanity, or to riots, or to superficial changes like straightening their hair, undergoing plastic eye, nose and breast surgery, and buying and applying tons of bleaching creams.

What have you really done? You have *destroyed* a part of *humanity*—a part of America, a part of you!''

While the majority of Sansei are mixing more freely with other racial groups than other Japanese Americans have done in the past, they still see many injustices and signs of potential trouble for all Japanese in the United States. The willingness of the Sansei to assert themselves to correct the inequities must surely help the Japanese Americans to achieve that American dream so eloquently stated by historian James Truslow Adams: ''. . . a land in which life should be better and richer and fuller for every man, with opportunity for each according to his ability or achievement.''[26]

11.
That Feeling
of Belonging

Some of the Issei remember the days in the late 1890s and early 1900s when the Japanese were not served in American restaurants or allowed in barber shops, hotels, and theaters. They saw crudely lettered signs saying "Japs, Keep Out!" on many establishments that were open to the general public. They were occasionally subject to physical abuse and frequently suffered slurs, indignities, and insults.

In this climate, the Japanese had no choice but to band together to achieve some power as a group. The Gentleman's Agreement, anti-alien laws, and the Immigration Act of 1924 were probably the most crucial single events affecting the growth of Japanese communities in America, for these acts were a direct display of American hostility. While the Japanese deeply resented this unfair treatment, they continued to desire success in America. Since the Japanese were unable to compete or receive fair treatment elsewhere, they began to rely on each other for trade. Thus, Japanese communities began to spring up.

The communities established by the Japanese provided not only a means of economic self-sufficiency, but also a source of group identity. They fulfilled the Japanese need to belong and to be a loyal member of a society. While the Japanese still retained the desire to be Americans, and hence accommodated themselves to American customs and values, their communities gave them a real group stability, a sense of "belonging" with other Japanese.

With their ability to organize and function as a group, the Japanese formed orderly communities which provided for each member. They also blended many skills to sponsor community activities attracting both young and old.

In this chapter we will take a look at some of the ways in which the Japanese maintained ''that feeling of belonging'' from the time the early immigrants came to the United States to the present day. As the times have changed, so have the ways in which people maintain a sense of community.

In the first decade of the twentieth century, numerous Japanese organizations, such as merchant and trade unions and prefecture groups, were operating on the West Coast. The prefecture groups, called *Kenjin-kai*, provided social and welfare aid for persons originating from that prefecture. In early times, they assisted needy persons, purchased boat tickets for the destitute desiring to return to Japan, and provided social activities for members. Today, their function is mainly limited to an annual picnic or dinner for all members and their relatives.

In the preceding chapter, the Japanese-operated gambling houses were mentioned. While the gambling clubs were illegal and constituted a black mark on the early Japanese record, they also served as a halfway house for many Japanese laborers who were barely making a living.

The Tokyo Club in Los Angeles provided two meals a day for migrant workers who passed through the city. After the evening meal, the innocent-looking dining area was transformed for gambling activities. A man who had worked as a delivery boy for one of the club's suppliers remembers what it was like.

> I used to deliver before the food was prepared at the club. I had to climb up to the third floor of a very steep stairway, lugging my eggs, bread and milk. It was always the same. As I approached the top step, there would be a guard sitting in a big, overstuffed chair. You could see a big revolver in a holster under his seat cushion. He would formally ask who I am and I'd say I'm the delivery boy from Embun. Then

he would knock at the door and warn the inside guard that the delivery boy is here. The door would open and I would be led through a narrow aisle to the kitchen. As I walked through the gambling section of the club, I used to see beautiful, innocent-looking card tables which were reversible and became crap tables or *shiko* (bean-counting) tables. At the cashier's cages, I'd see stacks of silver and gold coins. Noting the gleam in my eyes, the escorting guard would warn me to look straight ahead not sideways. "It's not good for young boys to gamble," he'd say every time. So I guess the gambling house had some moral advice for us youngsters.

While these clubs were illegal, they did give many men temporary shelters in America. When the men began to settle down, they joined the more durable Japanese community.

In the development of the Japanese community, the churches were in the forefront. Christian missions were established among the Japanese immigrants soon after their arrival in America. Buddhism, which was so important to many in Japan, served to retain the tie between the Japanese communities in America and their mother country. While Buddhist missionaries at first preached patriotism to Japan, a move which did not contribute to assimilation in America, the widespread criticism from both the American and the Japanese press brought about a change in their teachings.

Entertainment provided another means for the Japanese immigrants in the early days to get together and strengthen their emotional ties to their homeland. Nippon Kan in Seattle was typical of the theaters which, for all practical purposes, served as the centers of Japanese culture.

Nippon Kan was located in a hotel building, its unpretentious doorway was between the hotel entrance and the door to a grocery store. Inside, Nippon Kan was equally informal. Upstage on the left were the drummers, and on the extreme right were the *shamisen* (lute) players if a *kabuki* or some other

A scene from a kabuki, a Japanese play performed at Nippon Kan.

Japanese play was to be performed. On the extreme left was the *hanamichi* (runway) leading to the stage, which was built of wood. The ceiling was very high, so high, in fact, that the acoustics were not acoustics by any stretch of the imagination. The sounds bounced off in every direction.

While the performances were not free, instead of buying a ticket, one made a donation. Each *hana* (donation) was sealed in an envelope and handed to the receivers who jotted down the contribution. The donation was duly recorded in a book, and the name of the donor and the amount contributed were posted on a huge wall inside the hall. The contribution was normally doubled on paper to make an impression on other potential donors, but everyone knew that the figures were incorrect and made little sense.

An affair at Nippon Kan was a "night out" for families. While the children enjoyed themselves by racing up and down stairs from the main floor to the balcony, the adults met friends, exchanged pleasantries, and experienced in Nippon Kan a sense of belonging.

When the curtain rose to the rhythmic clap-clap of flat wooden sticks, Japanese eyes focused on Japanese performers. Audience-performer closeness was never more pronounced. Many of the entertainers were next-door neighbors.

The performances of these amateur entertainers ranged from mediocre to poor, falling far short of the skill displayed by their professional counterparts. The performers often forgot their lines, particularly when they stumbled onto words or phrases

A masked Nisei girl performing Modori bashi, a kabuki dance.

strange to their ordinary speech. They would then quickly improvise, sometimes with ingenious ease, but more often with ridiculous discomfort. Here, too, the unpaid amateur Hayakawas, Kamiyamas, and Aokis performed under considerable strain to the accompaniment of such uninspiring remarks as "Hey, isn't that so-and-so?" "Yeah, sure it is." "Gee, she looks funny." No one apologized or took the mistakes seriously. These home-grown entertainers had spent part of their spare time at work, at school, or at home rehearsing their lines, and a shortage of talent was more than offset by an abundance of spirit.

The traditional portion of the program was extremely popular with the Issei. Ancient Japanese plays, shamisen and *shakuhachi* (bamboo flute) players, and the classical odori pleased them most. The theme of many Japanese presentations was filial piety and the accompanying morality, and these were staged to impress the younger people. To the Issei, this was a time to recall Japan and recapture glimpses of that country's glorious past. For the younger set, there were entertainers such as harmonica players, vocalists, violinists, pianists, and comedians.

Today, Nippon Kan is silent. Similar situations prevail in other West Coast Japanese communities. The *engeikai* (entertainment programs), which were so much a part of Japanese community life, are but pleasant memories.

Not all forms of entertainment were Japanese in origin. The sports fans avidly followed the mighty feats of Babe Ruth and Lou Gehrig. They also took up baseball themselves.

When the Seattle-based Asahi and Mikado teams battled in the early 1920s, it was all-out war. Even before the first ball was tossed, the psychological warfare was on. In fact, one of the clubs once had the audacity to send a sword to the other, hinting that the members should use it if they lost the city's annual Japanese baseball championship game. Happily, mass hara-kiri never occurred.

During the Asahi-Mikado series, the Japanese community

was split into two camps. The fans took baseball seriously. Pennants and flags were flown, and lapel pins were worn to display loyalty to one or the other team.

The Asahi men's "clubhouse" was their coach's home. He even kept some of his star players in his home the night before a game. How he crammed them into his small home, no one knows. To start things off on the right pitch before an important game, he often bought a huge tuna fish to feed his men so that they would all be strong enough to play well.

As in Seattle, Japanese fans and teams in Los Angeles took baseball seriously. A Japanese tells about the time he was pitching for his team at an opponent's ball field. "You'd think I committed a murder. One of my pitches got away and hit an opposing batter. It was unintentional but the opposition and the fans were mad—mad enough to chase me out of the ball park. No, I didn't stick around, " he ruefully remembers, "It wasn't too healthy for me. I went home. Someone else finished up the ball game for me...."

Newspapers, at first printed entirely in Japanese and later, with sections in English, have expressed the changing interests and needs of the Japanese in the United States. In the first decades of the twentieth century, they were a means of fostering a feeling of belonging within the Japanese American community. In 1939, Shotaro Frank Miyamoto, a professor of sociology, commented on the importance of Japanese newspapers in unifying Japanese Americans.

> The solidarity of the [Japanese] community is promoted by the newspapers, primarily by the emphasis which they give to news which is essentially of Japanese or of their community interest; secondly, by any necessarily Japanese interpretation which they give to any general news; thirdly, through the efforts made by organizations to control the community through their columns; and finally, because their readers need not learn to read the American papers.[27]

How true that was when Japanese newspapers were aimed at the Japanese-reading Issei rather than the Nisei, whose knowledge of the Japanese language is limited.

With the addition of an English section to these Japanese newspapers, however, the editorial contents slowly took on a different position. The English sections began to articulate the achievements, the activities, and the attitudes of Japanese Americans in every field imaginable. Japanese were mentioned who otherwise would never have been noticed outside the narrow columns of their respective group bulletins or newsletters. The English sections gave the Japanese Americans a feeling that they belonged to a special group. The importance of these sections to the Japanese in America was expressed by a Nisei woman living in New York:

> We can always have access to ''regular'' news (city, state, international) but for issues and items pertaining specifically to the Japanese people, it must be presented by Japanese themselves. No one can speak for another ethnic group. Each group needs its own voice. Bilingual publications need not become passé. They can be a vital and enriching tie to bind us collectively as an ethnic group, and also reinforce an understanding of ourselves and other ethnic people, that we can be a viable political force capable of bringing changes that would benefit all.[28]

Many activities appealing to the Japanese in America have undergone quite a change. In pre-World War II days, few Japanese thought anything of driving miles to attend a dance sponsored by one of their own groups. Motoring down a highway on a Saturday afternoon for an evening dance and returning home the next morning were not uncommon. Today, few organizations sponsor dances, for dances no longer serve to draw many people together and are usually limited in interest to the members of a particular organization.

Conventions have now become important in the social life of many Japanese Americans. One of the largest of these in the

Northwest is sponsored by the Northwest Young Buddhist League. The program includes discussions, an oratorical contest, a dance, and bowling and basketball tournaments. Group discussions normally are extremely diverse, running from boy-girl relationships and Buddhism to such topics as "Whither to, the Japanese?" The oratorical contests produce eloquent speakers expounding the beauty of Buddhism and its value in life.

Japanese engaged in specific occupations, such as medicine or gardening, often have their own associations. Women are usually the stronger supporters of traditional Japanese culture. They frequently join classes in Japanese dancing, flower arrangement, classical singing, origami, poetry, the playing of koto, tea ceremony, bonsai, and even Japanese character writing. There are also clubs where Japanese may play *goh* (Japanese stone piece game), *shogi* (Japanese chess), and bridge. A post-World War II organization that has gained wide acceptance is the *Hyakunen-kai* (One-Hundred-Year Club). Membership is extended to those desiring to live to age one hundred. The Japanese also have community service groups which entertain visiting dignitaries and scholars from Japan. These groups also call on sick Issei who have no relatives and sometimes offer counsel to individual Japanese.

The important contributions of the JACL to the welfare of Japanese Americans during World War II have been discussed previously. Today, the JACL continues to maintain its position as the guardian of Japanese American rights. As a national Asian American organization, the JACL is also aware of its duty to the larger Asian American community. To meet the challenging social and economic changes in the nation, the JACL has brought into its fold a host of disciplines ranging from political science, law, and mass communication to education and public administration. JACL representatives have served in national agencies such as the Office of Health, Education and Welfare (HEW), and in major federal functions like the White House Conference on Aging and the American Immigration and Citizenship Conference.

While the JACL sponsors many activities that have been mentioned earlier, such as dances and conventions, the organization is concentrating more on encouraging people to become involved in large-scale social, political, and economic matters. The JACL has formed committees to develop educational materials on Japanese Americans and to sponsor events and programs for parents and grandparents in their retirement years.

At this writing, there are 96 JACL chapters comprising over 27,000 members residing in 32 states. In addition to regional offices, the JACL maintains an office in the nation's capital to initiate legislation in the interest of Japanese Americans, to watch for federal programs affecting Asian Americans, and to report political trends to the local chapters. Indeed, the JACL is cognizant of employment discrimination against Asian Americans in both the blue and white collar labor ranks.

A giant step forward for the JACL was the formation of the JAY (Japanese American Youth). This group is aimed at developing leadership and organizational skills among the younger Japanese Americans through workshops, conferences, and community projects. Recognizing the JAYs as future leaders, the JACL is counting on them for new directions and programs to fill the needs and aspirations of Japanese Americans.

12.
The Church-Goers

Most Japanese are guided by the golden legacies left by Gautama Buddha and Jesus Christ. The Japanese use the teachings of these two great religious leaders to help direct them in their everyday behavior. The difference in lifestyle between Buddhist Japanese Americans and the Christian Japanese Americans is the difference in their observance of their respective religions. Whereas Christian Japanese Americans are comfortable in a Christian-oriented American society, Buddhist Japanese Americans sometimes find themselves in an awkward situation on such Christian holidays as Christmas. But the Buddhist Japanese Americans have learned to adjust by taking advantage of this holiday season to join their Christian Japanese Americans in the spirit of giving and exchanging gifts. That is the only clearly visible difference between the two groups—a difference similar to that between Americans of other religious faiths. They are Americans first, away from their churches.

Both Buddhism and Christianity had been long practiced in Japan before the Japanese began immigrating to the United States. Buddhism came to Japan over fourteen hundred years ago with the spread of Chinese civilization. While the Japanese adopted Buddhism, the form of that religion was profoundly altered by Shinto, the earliest religion in Japan, and one which has had far-reaching effects on the Japanese character. Associated with Shinto is the traditional Japanese devotion to nature. The beliefs of Shinto are confined to the here and now.

Buddhism in Japan, while embracing the concept of an afterlife, allows for the Japanese concern for the present and love of nature. Much of the Indian mysticism in traditional Buddhism has been eliminated to accommodate Shinto beliefs.

Christianity was introduced to Japan in 1549 when St. Francis Xavier, a Jesuit missionary, baptized nearly one thousand converts during a twenty-six month sojourn. By 1582 there were at least 150,000 converts.

Why were the Japanese attracted to Christianity? Otis Cary, D.D., in *A History of Christianity in Japan*,[29] tells of an incident which, no doubt, contributed towards Xavier's phenomenal success. Xavier asked Anjiro, a man he met in Malacca, if he went to Japan, whether the people would become Christians. Anjiro replied,

> My people would not immediately become Christians; but they would first ask you a multitude of questions, weighing carefully your answers and your claims. Above all, they would observe whether your conduct agreed with your words. If you should satisfy them on these points—by suitable replies to their inquiries and by a life above reproach—then, as soon as the matter was known and fully examined, the king [daimyo], the nobles, and the educated people would become Christians. Six months would suffice; for the nation is one that always follows the guidance of reason.

The year Xavier reached Japan, the Buddhist priests held the greatest political power in the nation. The fact that some Buddhist monks were exerting their influence in politics for personal and partisan advantages created an unhappy state of affairs. Feudal lords also jostled for power. Nobunaga, a man who deplored the senseless power struggles, was a prime mover for a centralized government. Cary notes,

> Of natural consequences, those who desired powers for themselves were ready to welcome whatever seemed likely to weaken that of Buddhism. This is

> doubtless the chief reason why Nobunaga [Oda]
> showed such favour to the missionaries; and it had
> much to do with the readiness of many feudal lords to
> receive into their territories the men whom they
> hoped to utilize as instruments for diminishing the
> arrogance of the Buddhist priests.[30]

Among the early converts were the princes of Amakusa, Arima, Bungo, and Omura. After they had been converted, the princes had no difficulty inducing their feudal subjects to follow their example.

At first, Japanese rulers did not oppose Christianity, though they recognized the Christians' allegiance to the Pope as a threat to Japanese stability. However, by 1587, the Tokugawa government decided that Christian missionaries might very well be early signs of a Western invasion of Japan. To maintain national unity, the government resolved to eliminate Christianity. This decision was to lead to one of the worst religious persecutions ever recorded in the history of Japan.

The records indicate that at least 200,000 Japanese Christians were persecuted from 1629 to 1872. The largest mass arrest in Japanese history, known as the *Uragami Kuzure*, took place during 1867-1880. It is said that this mass arrest was inspired by the visit of Commodore Perry. Freedom for these Japanese Christians was made possible in 1883 through joint protests by Catholics and Protestants in America and England.

Because the number of Christians in Japan had been greatly reduced by long-standing government policies, most Japanese immigrants in the United States were initially Buddhists, and they brought their native rituals with them. However, as these immigrants were eager to become Americanized, and as the Buddhist Church was not organized in America until the end of the nineteenth century, a large percentage of the Issei were converted to Christianity. Christian workers were often instrumental in helping the Japanese find jobs and learn about America. This naturally brought many Japanese in contact with the churches.

The Japanese Christian experience in the United States started in 1879 with the formation of the Japanese Gospel Society *(Fukuin Kai)* in San Francisco. In the beginning, the Japanese Christian churches served as night schools to teach English so the young immigrants might learn to speak and behave like other Americans. As Dr. Paul Nagano, a Baptist minister from Los Angeles, says:

> Growth among the churches was not primarily due to the various theological emphases. The physical convenience of the church, the attractiveness of the minister and the program of the church offered, and the desire to be near one's friends seem to have been more important in drawing Issei to the various churches. For most of them, a Christian church was a Christian church, and never mind the nuances of theology.

After World War II, the policy of almost every major Protestant denomination was to do away with the segregated Japanese ethnic churches. An effort was made by the churches to assimilate the Japanese Americans who had returned from internment camps, the Midwest, and the East Coast. Several denominations — for example, the Methodists and the Baptists — closed some of their ethnic churches. A Japanese American Methodist pastor expresses the feelings behind this policy:

> It will be necessary for a church to be involved in the entire community, not just in an ethnic community. So far, the church has been somewhat irrelevant to what is really going on in the world. She must be involved if she is to be effective in her work at all.

Assimilation, however, was not entirely successful. Established churches were unprepared, and Japanese Americans were hesitant. It was inevitable that the pre-World War II pattern of small denominational Japanese Christian churches would again develop in the Japanese communities. A revival of the ethnic church has occurred in the last few years. The Japanese vicar of an Episcopal church on the West Coast comments on the Japanese Christian and Buddhist churches:

> The ''ethnic'' church appears to be necessary at this
> stage of church life insofar as we seem to be living in
> a ''race-conscious'' climate since the late 1960s and
> the present decade [1970s]. Until the racial stratifica-
> tion of society changes appreciably, it would seem
> that people need to be ministered to in the context of
> society as it is presently structured. Racial identity
> cannot be ignored in ministering to people as per-
> sons.

While the Japanese churches naturally emphasize purely religious work, these churches are becoming more aware of the
importance of social and recreational activities to the Sansei.
Camp Fire Girls, Boy Scouts, parties, athletics, and dances are
a part of church activities. Bazaars and conventions are also high
on the church agenda. Some bazaars are huge events: a traditional Labor Day event sponsored by a Buddhist church in one
western city often requires more than a ton of rice for the
Japanese delicacies. The women rise as early as four o'clock in
the morning to make *sushi* and *ohagi* for this bazaar.

The Nisei are making an effort at exposing their youngsters,
the Sansei, to an environment of discipline and meditation which
are very much a part of any church. As was mentioned earlier in
the book, many Nisei are bent on introducing their youngsters to
other Sansei, and the churches provide an opportunity for the
Sansei to meet. While a few Sansei attend church services
because they are persuaded to do so by their parents, most
Sansei go on their own because they see the value of church
attendance in their own growth.

While the Japanese churches have become somewhat
Americanized, the Buddhist churches have tended to retain a
link with Japan. It is here that many receive instruction in
Japanese ways. Recently, there has been a revival of interest in
Japanese customs, and the services, funerals, visitations, and
temple tours show distinct Japanese influence. The weddings,
once in the Western tradition, today use Buddhist vows and
Buddhist music.

The Buddhist church's link with Japan could be likened to the Catholic church's ties with the Vatican in Italy. Neither of them is likely to sever its relations with the mother church. In the case of the Buddhist churches in the United States, their members are mostly Japanese. If the Buddhist churches are becoming Westernized, that should come as no surprise. Buddhist churches in other lands have conformed to the language and culture of those countries. Nor should it be surprising that the Buddhist churches in the United States are taking a long, hard look at themselves with an eye on building a solid foundation for the future. A Buddhist priest takes this view of his church's future:

There are many parents here who not only bring their children to our Sunday School activities but also take in religiously oriented functions, such as religious services, Buddhist cultural activities and other occasions of Buddhist activities.

It is true that the absolute number of our Sunday School children shows a decrease every year. But there is a lot of activity in our temple aimed at other English-speaking adults, one of them being our weekly lecture sessions on Buddhism.

Our Japanese Issei services have a large number of regular devotees and this is one area in which we hope not to see a great drop in attendance and participation.

The Japanese Buddhist churches' survival depends now on the continued interest and support of the Issei and Nisei and surely later the Sansei and succeeding generations. That is the reason Buddhist churches are concentrating on breaking down the language barrier, for one, to accommodate the growing number of Sansei. Basically, all Buddhists try to follow the teachings handed down by Gautama Buddha.

An outsider finds an aura of mystery surrounding Buddhism as a religion and a philosophy of life. Buddhism is not something one can learn in a few easy lessons. Space prevents a thorough examination of Buddhism. Mrs. Sita Renfrew of Boston has succeeded, nevertheless, in explaining some of the key points of

Buddhism in meaningful terms. In "A Buddhist Guide for Laymen," published by the Cambridge [Mass.] Buddhist Association, Inc., she writes in part:

> In Buddhism, the individual is largely the architect of his spiritual structure: he can seek guidance and instruction, but when he acts it has to be entirely of his own volition and with the full understanding that he, and he alone, can be held accountable for the resulting consequences. No monk or spiritual leader can ever command the conscience of a Buddhist, however humble such may be.
>
> Buddhism enlightens its adherents as to the real nature of the universe, including the laws and forces operating therein. Buddhism discloses to the earnest seeker the essence of his being, showing him the true nature of the higher destiny which extends beyond this fleeting earth-life. By awakening his slumbering moral forces and faculties, it [Buddhism] kindles in him a desire for the good and noble and true; thus he seeks to become humane, patient, unselfish, and enduring, thereby gaining understanding of life's sorrows, confidence in his ultimate destiny, and courage to seek the highest aim of every living being: emancipation, consummation, Nibbana [Nirvana, the state of Errorlessness].

And, Mrs. Renfrew adds, Buddhism is also a philosophy since it "demands of its adherents not blind faith in any God-Creator, but a personal conviction gained and confirmed by one's own investigation, examination, and experimentation in dealing with facts as they exist." In other words, she is saying that the precepts of Buddhism are not based upon the will of a Supreme Being, nor upon the pronouncements of religious leaders. "Instead," Mrs. Renfrew continues, "the natural constitution of the world and of life as we experience it are freely studied and investigated in order to become enlightened, resulting in a life so lived that the least harm results to self and fellow beings."

In Buddhism, sorrow is thought to be ever present and everywhere. It is the result of uncontrolled desires or attachments. Emancipation from sorrow is possible by following the eightfold path: Right comprehension that dissipates delusion; right aspiration that hurts no one; right speech that makes for clarity; right conduct that brings no regret; right livelihood that causes no discredit; right endeavor that results in goodness; right self-discipline that gives controlled action; and right awareness that leads to Nirvana. Buddhism is also a way of life which, the Buddhists contend, assures one a sense of inner peace and security.

Just as there are Christian holidays and Jewish holidays, Buddhists also have their holidays. One of the most important dates is April 8—Buddha Day (*Hanamatsuri*). On that day, a service is held to commemorate the birth of Gautama in Lumbini Garden. Bishop Takashi Tsuji once described the rite in this manner:

> During the service a flower shrine known as Hanamido is set up in front of the main shrine as a symbol of Lumbini Garden. In this shrine is placed a statuette of the infant Buddha and the congregation offers flowers and pours sweet tea over the image. According to the ancient legend, the universe was filled with joyful music, flowers bloomed in full glory and sweet rain fell from the heavens to make this a joyful event.

Two other significant Buddhist holidays are January 16, Shinran Shonin Memorial Day (*Ho-on-ko*), and September 1, BCA (Buddhist Churches of America) Founding Day (*Beikoku Bukkyo Kaikyo Kinenbi*). Ho-on-ko, meaning a gathering to express Buddhist gratitude, is a service in memory of Shinran Shonin (May 21, 1173—January 16, 1262), the founder of Buddhism's *Jodo Shin Shu* (True Pure Land Sect). Beikoku Bukkyo Kaikyo Kinenbi is the day marking the official introduction of Jodo Shin Shu into the mainland United States on September 1, 1899.

Another widely celebrated Buddhist event is the *Bon Odori*, a holiday which fascinates many non-Japanese and non-Buddhists. Tiny Sansei children in colorful kimonos join young people and adults dancing in streets lighted by lanterns. While the Bon Odori is a time for rejoicing, it is essentially a memorial observance in which homage and respect are paid to the dead. As one expresses gratitude for the return of the deceased's spirit, thought is directed toward their virtues, endeavors, deeds, and life, all of which affected the heritage left the living. With the thoughts thus oriented, attention is focused on the oneness of the past, present, and future, on interdependency and harmony of all existence, on the workings of the karma, and on cause and effect which manifest all that is life. The aim of this reflection is to produce a fuller awareness and understanding of life. Not only Sansei students of religion, but also many young non-Japanese, see Buddhism as an important philosophy of life.

Youngsters attending Bon Odori festivities take time out for something to eat.

At Bon Odori in Seattle, Washington, the drummer (upper right) keeps time for those in the procession, while others watch from the sidelines.

Mrs. Hugh McLeod, a non-Japanese woman who is a member of a Buddhist church, cites these views for the increase in Caucasian acceptance of Buddhism:

> Buddhism is logical, reasonable. It makes known the law of cause and effect which pervades all life, beings, worlds. This, in turn, is logical, just, and answers seemingly unsolvable questions.
>
> Buddhism explains how life is like a wheel that turns round and round, with man living again and again until he has come to see life as it is rather than the way he should like it to be.
>
> Buddhism teaches us to live a code of ethics, not for our own gain, or even for realizing Buddhahood, but for the sake of all that live. Buddhism shows the necessity of putting into practice the great Bodhisattva ideal of truly caring about one another. All beings are intertwined with one having some sort of effect upon all.
>
> There is no fear in Buddhism. Buddhism is tolerant. It tells us that there are many paths to the summit of Infinite Truth. You may take one path, and I may take another, but eventually we will all come to see life aright.

On October 26, 1967, the noted American artist, Richard C. Kirsten, was ordained a Zen Buddhist priest and given the name Daiensai Kuden Bon Sekidojin in the Zuisenji Zen Temple in Kamakura, Japan. Since then, Kirsten has been signing all his paintings and prints with both his Western and Eastern names. This is Kirsten's explanation of how he became acquainted with Zen:

> I did not seek Zen. Zen found me. Zen produces an understanding of nature and man—and my place in the cosmos. Zen awakens the intuitive forces which play the most important factor for any creative art. Zen, through an understanding of meditation and silence and solitude, brings a peace and understand-

ing that is a more unitarian approach to man's relationship to humanity. Zen embraces religious and philosophical concepts of spirituality but does not overlook the necessity of the mundane. Zen taught me that it isn't just painting and sculpture, music or drama that is art—but that *all* of life and all of man's senses is *art*. Zen teaches transcendence in all facets of life and living—not just in the spirit but in thought and deed. Only in experiencing Zen can Zen be realized. But Zen can be found anywhere in the world. It isn't necessary to seek it in Buddhist temples but can be experienced in meditation and in transcendent thought and action. Zen is self-awareness and Zen is self-discipline, silence, solitude and the total awareness of cosmic forces in the realm of mystic thought energies.

Mrs. McLeod and Mr. Kirsten are but two of many Caucasians who have discovered particular aspects of Buddhism to their liking. They are pioneers of a sort; that is, they are embracing a great but misunderstood religion. If their views are indicative of those held by other non-Japanese Buddhists, then it is safe to predict Buddhism has a chance of not only surviving but growing in a nation which offers religious freedom to everyone.

13.
The Funeral

Almost every Japanese funeral has a touch of old Japan. The Japanese have a penchant for custom. The ritual of each funeral must be as exact and delicate as each stroke of a Japanese character written on an unblemished sheet of paper. The Japanese take funeral attendance seriously. A Japanese person would even go to a casual friend's funeral. The Japanese feel strongly about social obligations and relationships, and they often express compassion for people which transcends the usual conventions of friendship.

Up through the time of the Depression, a go-between handled all matters pertaining to a death instead of the family. The funeral director was contacted by the head of an organization such as a prefecture group or social club to which the deceased had belonged. Few Japanese Americans now use go-betweens, and the Nisei are assuming the duties of these family affairs.

Before World War II, most Japanese preferred cremation to burial. The reason for this was understandable. Since they had lived their formative years in Japan and were not allowed to become citizens of their adopted country, Japan was home. The Issei wanted to have their ashes taken to Japan. The passage of the Walter-McCarran Immigration and Naturalization Act in 1952 has enabled a sizable number of Issei to become naturalized American citizens. The passage of years has also weakened emotional ties with Japan. Thus more and more people, especially the Nisei, favor burials today.

When there is a death in the family, a death announcement is published in a Japanese language newspaper in a black-bordered, boxed notice. The date for the funeral is set several days later so that non-English-speaking Japanese will have time to learn of the death.

The funeral service is usually held at night, a custom which dates back to the time when the whole Japanese community worked during the day, and people couldn't afford to stay away from their jobs to attend funerals.

Christian funerals follow the customs of the West, although the service is conducted in Japanese. We will take a look at the Buddhist funeral services, which consist of traditional Japanese rites.

A funeral at a Buddhist temple tends to be an elaborate, very Japanese affair. Each person attending the funeral brings with him an envelope containing money to leave at the *koden* desk, which is normally located at the entrance of the temple. Koden is a monetary offering made for the purchase of incense. The receiver—*uketsuke*, as the Japanese call him—accepts the donation, records its amount, and in return offers the bereaved family's envelope which has either a handkerchief or stamps tucked inside. This is a Japanese gesture of reciprocity with grateful thanks.

Large floral wreaths are placed on either side of the altar. The casket is brought into the church by the pallbearers. Then the priest leads the way down the center aisle toward the altar, followed by the honorary pallbearers. Behind them are the pallbearers with the casket, followed by family members. The family sits on the left side in the front row; and the pallbearers, on the right.

The strong smell of burning incense and an air of sadness fill the church as the priest chants antiphonally the *sutras* (scripture narratives) relating to the dead. He periodically strikes a gong during his chanting. Sorrow etched on their faces, the family members sit in silent grief. Their heads bowed, they say their prayers with a string of beads in their hands.

During the second sutra chant, the immediate family, relatives, pallbearers, and friends walk up to the casket, bow, and then burn incense before returning to their seats. One doubts if the majority of the people understand the priest. After all, he is pronouncing words in a language strange and archaic to the ears of the average Japanese. But who can deny the beauty of the mysterious and unknown? The mood is keyed to the solemnity and gravity over the loss of a fellow human being.

Eulogies presented by the priest emphasize the brightest side of the deceased's life. Incense offerings by a representative of a club or the community follow the eulogies. If the deceased was a civic figure or a club officer, the representative recites his accomplishments and praises his role in various activities. After the acknowledgment by a member of the bereaved family, the mourners move toward the casket and bow their heads in token of a final *sayonara* to the one who has left them. Then the casket is closed, and the funeral cortege, led by the priest, leaves the sanctuary in the same order it went to the altar.

The service concluded, the veil of politeness is slowly lowered. Men gather in small knots to chat in hushed voices, and the women, bowing and bowing to one another, also talk among themselves. There was a time when a dinner was considered necessary after a funeral. This was an *arigato* (thank you) to those who were considerate and kind enough to help the bereaved family in its hour of grief. The custom, however laudable, is losing its hold on the Japanese. The current substitute for a dinner is a box lunch or a package of tea to take home.

Sometimes, Buddhist funeral services are held in the home before a family altar that is flanked by sprays of flowers, scrolls, and name tablets. There is always burning incense. The picture of the deceased occupies a dominant position in the center of the altar table. Many Japanese Buddhists still continue the practice of keeping ancestor tablets in household shrines and giving daily offerings of food and drink to their dead and to Buddha.

Some time after the funeral, the Buddhist priest holds memorial services in honor of the deceased, for sorrow casts a long shadow into the lives of Buddhists who faithfully remember their dead. Instead of koden, *Ohkumotsu* (an offering, usually a bean jam bun) is offered at the memorial service.

A devout Buddhist is truly dedicated to the custom of remembering the dead. Years and years ago, Buddhists went through the condolences in a rather leisurely, relaxed manner — visiting, sipping tea or sake, and offering condolences. Times have changed, and so has the tempo of life. But these changes have not changed the ways in which some Japanese still carry on their ways of belief and worship in time of sorrow.

To a non-Japanese, it may seem odd that there are no tears shed at a Japanese funeral. "Do not burden others with your sorrow," is an injunction of self-control practiced by the Japanese. In public, the bereaved try to keep their heartbreak and inner turmoil to themselves.

Although he is writing about Japan in *Japanese People and Politics,*[31] Chitosi Yanaga well expresses the stoicism with which Japanese Americans react to personal loss.

> ...The concealment of anxiety and grief is as natural as the control of one's temper and not unlike the Englishman's phlegm. But behind such rigid control lies a stronger emotion than behind the habitual outbursts of a more volatile people....Beneath the rather solid surface of stoicism is found the sentimental, emotional make-up of the Japanese which shows up so clearly once the barrier is penetrated.

The decorum of the bereaved, the obligations which they feel toward honoring the deceased, and the courtesy and compassion with which family members are treated by the larger community point up a characteristic trait of the Japanese in America.

14.
It's Not All Sukiyaki

When anyone is asked what he or she knows about Japanese food, invariably the first word blurted out is *sukiyaki*, which is a Japanese stew. *Suki* means "spade" or "shovel," and *yaki* means "broiled." So sukiyaki is "shovel-broiled" or "spade-broiled."

Buddhist teaching forbade the killing and eating of birds and animals. Believing that their dead return to earth in another form of life, the Buddhists felt that one might be feasting on the reincarnation of an ancestor—or maybe a distant relative. The Japanese farmer in the field, however, put hunger above religion and cooked meat and vegetables on his iron spade over an open fire.

The first sukiyaki restaurant was started by a barkeeper named Jimbei in Yokohama late in the Edo period (around 1600). Jimbei, the story goes, wanted to open a sukiyaki restaurant, but his wife did not like the idea of an eatery specializing in meat which was taboo to those who faithfully followed the Buddhist religion. Her reluctance may also have been buttressed by the fact that she had a prosperous noodle stand.

Jimbei and his wife compromised by erecting a partition in their tiny shop. Jimbei served sukiyaki and sake on his side, and his wife dished out noodles on her side. Eventually, the sukiyaki-sake business was more successful. The partition inside the shop came down, and the sukiyaki sign went up outside. Jimbei's wife quit selling noodles, joined her husband, and together they prospered in business.

The Veleda Club, an organization affiliated with the Young Women's Christian Association and comprised of Japanese-American women in Portland, Oregon, has this recipe for sukiyaki. It serves five people.

1 pound tender beef
Suet or 2 tablespoons fat
1 can yam noodles
8 to 10 green onions with tops
1 cake *tofu* (bean curd), cut in squares
5 eggs (optional)
3 tablespoons sugar
¼ cup *shoyu* (Japanese soy sauce)
½ tablespoon *ajinomoto* (vegetable protein derivative)
1 tablespoon *sake*

Slice beef crossgrain, paper-thin. Cut green onions, including the green tops, diagonally, about 1½ inches long. Arrange all ingredients—meat, yam noodles, green onions, and tofu— in separate piles on a large platter. Make sauce by combining sugar, shoyu, ajinomoto, and sake. Heat only to dissolve sugar.

Melt suet in heated skillet and cover bottom of pan with slices of meat.

Cook only until partially done, and place to one side of pan. Add yam noodles, green onions, and tofu. Pour on enough sauce to cover all ingredients and cook over high heat, turning frequently to hasten cooking.

Transfer the meat to the top of the other ingredients to prevent overcooking. Lower heat and continue cooking without stirring—only until onions are tender. Do not overcook. Sukiyaki should be eaten when ingredients are barely done—adding meat, vegetables, and sauce to the pan as it [each ingredient] is taken out.

Sukiyaki meat is flavorful when it is either rare or well done. Therefore, while sukiyaki is cooking, diners may spoon out their choice of food into individual dishes and eat it with a bowl of hot rice. The real gourmet dips the sukiyaki into a raw beaten egg. The egg is considered a delicacy and is also nutritious.

The following sauce "makes" the sukiyaki:

½ cup water plus a bouillon cube or two
¼ cup soy sauce
¾ tablespoon sake or sauterne
2 tablespoons sugar

Besides sukiyaki, another Japanese favorite is *teriyaki*. A friend passes along this teriyaki recipe:

2 pounds top sirloin steak, sliced thin and diagonally
2 teaspoons grated fresh ginger
1 clove garlic, grated
1 medium onion, chopped fine
1 teaspoon ajinomoto
¼ cup Japanese soy sauce
¼ cup sugar
½ cup sake

Mix all the ingredients (except the meat). Cook over low heat, stirring constantly until sugar is dissolved and boiling point is reached. Cool. Pour this teriyaki sauce over meat and marinate for an hour. Drain. Thread the meat on bamboo skewers and broil 3 to 5 minutes, turning once, preferably over charcoal. Baste with the sauce while cooking.

Who among connoisseurs of Japanese food would let you forget *tempura*? This delicacy is usually made of *ebi* (shrimp) or bits of fish or vegetables dipped in batter, cooked in oil, and served hot with a side dish of steaming rice. Isao Yabuki, in *Foods of Tokyo*, writes,

There are various ways of eating tempura—but in all of them it should be hot. Usually, tempura is served with dashi (broth of soy sauce) and a supplementary dish of daikon oroshi (grated radish) and shoga (ginger root). Some foreigners like it with salt and lemon juice—in Western style. Others like tendon (bowl of hot rice with fried fish and sauce atop it).[32]

Tempura isn't all that Japanese. The name tempura derives from the Portuguese *tempuras*, or Ember days for fasting. The origin of the dish goes back to the time of the first white missionaries who came to Nagasaki before Japan was opened wide to the Western world. On days when the missionaries refrained from eating meat, they substituted fish coated in batter and cooked in deep oil. The Nagasaki Japanese liked the taste, and before long, they adopted tempura as their own.

Preparing tempura is an art. Yakubi continues:

As in ancient days, when Masamune, the famed swordsmith, forged a blade, he plunged the heated iron into water of an exact temperature. So it is with tempura. The cooking oil should be at 170-180 degrees for the whole cooking period. The best proportions are: one egg beaten, four times the egg's bulk of cold water, five times the egg's bulk of flour. Beat egg and water together well, add the flour all at once and mix rapidly—a French whip is best for it.

Coat the raw food with the batter, drop into the heated oil, cook until golden brown, and lift out to drain on soft paper. Too much flour makes tempura doughy and not crisp; oil too hot makes the crust tough. Delay in serving makes it soft and unpalatable.

The foods listed below may give the reader an idea of the wide selection of Japanese dishes.

Traditional Japanese meat dishes include beef teriyaki (barbecued beef steak with teriyaki sauce), beef *shioyaki* (beef steak broiled with salt), *tonkatsu* (pork loin—Japanese style), and sukiyaki (beef with seasonal vegetables, soybean curd, mushrooms, scallions, and bamboo shoots).

Popular dishes are *nabe-mono* (food cooked in a flat pan)

which includes *udon-suki* (meat, shrimp, chicken, vegetables with noodles), *kani-nabe* (crab in broth with vegetables), chicken *mizutaki* (tender chicken in broth with vegetables), *niku-dofu* (beef and bean cake), *buta-dofu* (pork and bean cake), and *yu-dofu* (warm bean cake).

Some forms of sushi (dishes with raw fish and rice dipped in soy sauce mixed with mustard paste) are *nigiri, tekka-maki, kappa-maki, futo-maki,* and *tekka-donburi*. Sushi is a favorite among Japanese, and in 1900 there were many *sushiyas* (sushi restaurants) on the West Coast.

Other Japanese foods are *awabi shiomushi* (steamed abalone), *kani sunomono* (crab meat salad with vinegar), *sugaki* (oysters seasoned with vinegar), *kazu-konbu* (herring roe on seaweed), *suzuko* (salmon roe), *oyako-ae* (pickled salmon), *tarako* (cod roe), *yakko-dofu* (cold bean cake), *yakinori* (seaweed), *rakkyo* (pickled onions), *oshitashi* (boiled greens with seasoned soy sauce dressing), *sumashi* (clear soup), *misoshiru* (bean soup), *oshinko* (special Japanese pickle), *mochi* (rice cake), *manju* (bean jam bun), and *ohagi* (rice cake covered with sweet beans).

Every Japanese restaurant has a special formal dinner. One example would be: *tsukidashi* (hors d'oeuvres), *sashimi* (sliced raw fish), *sunomono* (Japanese salad with vinegar dressing), *misoshiru* (bean soup) or *sumashi* (clear soup), *nimono* (steamed Japanese dish), *yakimono* (broiled Japanese dish), tempura (deep fried prawns, fish, and vegetables), rice, tea, and *tsukemono* (pickled vegetables). And, would you believe it, ice cream—the added American touch!

Seafood prepared by the Japanese includes oysters (deep fried), salmon teriyaki or shioyaki (salmon with teriyaki sauce or salmon broiled with salt), *sakamushi* (fish steamed in sake), *saba shioyaki* (mackerel broiled with salt), *sashimi* (sliced raw fish), *yamakake* (raw fish topped with Japanese yam), *kani* (crab with sauce), *kujira* (whale), and *unagi* (charcoal-broiled eels).

The dishes made with chicken are chicken teriyaki (barbecued chicken with teriyaki sauce), and chicken shioyaki (tender chicken broiled with salt).

One of the "musts" in eating Japanese food is the proper use of chopsticks. Most Japanese Americans, especially the Nisei, learned from childhood how to handle chopsticks. Even so, they had their problems. For instance, one young fellow tried using a pair of chopsticks to pick up a piece of sparerib at a banquet. The piece slipped onto the plate of the man sitting next to him. Luckily, the man was looking the other way and was engrossed in loud conversation with a friend. He later consumed the fugitive sparerib.

Slurping soup is not considered good manners in the Western world. In the Japanese society, however, slurping soup delights the hosts, for it is a way of telling them that the soup is delicious and that you are enjoying it immensely.

The popularity of Japanese food rose after World War II. The introduction of Japanese food to the American occupation forces opened an entirely new spectrum of tastes to many soldiers and to those who followed them to Japan. These people returned to the states and sought out Japanese *meshiyas* (restaurants), which, as a result, have sprung up all over the United States.

Right after the war, when the people of Japan could barely afford to eat, such delicacies as bamboo shoots, dried mushrooms, seaweed, and *kazunoko* (herring roe) were flown to the United States by the tons to earn U.S. dollars for devastated Japan. Of course, there was much disapproval expressed by postwar visitors from Japan when they saw, in the United States, Japanese foodstuffs not displayed at stores in their own country.

Today, live eels are flown in plastic bags of water to cities throughout the world. There are classes in Japanese cooking for those who want to learn more about the art of preparing Japanese foods. Every ingredient needed for Japanese dishes is within reach at a grocery store or a supermarket. It is easy to see why the tremendous flow of Japanese foodstuffs amounts to a million-dollar business each year.

The preparation of a sukiyaki dinner, followed by the pleasure of eating it.

New York leads the way in elegant Japanese restaurants. On the West Coast, the center for Japanese eating places is Los Angeles. While many Japanese restaurants are partially Westernized, some are truly Japanese. Low-bowing, graceful Japanese waitresses, always at one's beck and call, greet each customer with: *"Ah, yoku-irrasshai-mashita! Dozo, kochira-e!"* (Very glad you came. This way, please.) The diners slip off their shoes and sit knees-down on a *tatami* (a straw mat), before a low table. Dinner is served!

Epilogue

"Dad, tell me something about the Japanese," the young girl asked her father.

So the father sat down at his desk, inserted a white sheet of paper into the typewriter, and began to write *The Japanese American Story*.

First, he took her across the Pacific Ocean to trace their ancestry. Who the Japanese were and where they came from were questions that needed explanation in order to place the Japanese American story in its proper perspective.

Then, the father and his daughter returned to the United States and traveled the various roads that the Japanese immigrants had taken to find a place they can call home.

Like some of their European counterparts, the Japanese immigrants faced hostility and discrimination. This portion of the early immigrants' story had to be told so the father and his daughter could continue a meaningful journey in their search for the truth about the Japanese.

The journey was marked with rivers of tears—tears of joy in discovering the heart of America, in saluting the heroism of the Japanese American soldiers, in appreciating the beauty of Japanese culture—and tears of sorrow in reliving the hurt of concentration camps.

In retrospect, the Japanese, having endured the ordeal of Executive Order 9066 which sent them to so-called "relocation centers," hope such a wholesale evacuation never visits any other group in America. The United States, it should be pointed out, acknowledged evacuation claims, however token the payment.

A delightful trend in American society is its acceptance of Japanese flower arrangement, bonsai, and art, but the final reward of this journey for the father and his daughter was that it gave them a better insight into their people.

Notes

1. As quoted by Franz H. Michael and George E. Taylor in *The Far East in the Modern World* (New York: Henry Holt, 1956), p. 254.

2. Naomi Egami, "Equestrian Tribes from Korea," *The East* 4 (1968): 15.

3. Japanese American Research Project, University of California at Los Angeles.

4. Hisakazu Kaneko, *Manjiro: The Man Who Discovered America* (Boston: Houghton Mifflin, 1956), p. 137.

5. Letter to author.

6. February 24, 1942, Japanese American Archives, University of Washington.

7. *Seattle Times,* February 28, 1942.

8. *Seattle Times,* March 1, 1942.

9. *Seattle Times,* March 2, 1942.

10. Tacoma, Wash. Learning Center, Fort Steilacoom Community College. "Evacuation and Camp Life."

11. Harry Honda, *Pacific Citizen,* December 17, 1971.

12. As summarized by Dr. Kitano in letter to author, January 1, 1974.

13. Chester Rowell, *San Francisco Chronicle,* February 1, 1943.

14. *Press Democrat,* January 29, 1943.

15. *Northwest Times,* November 1, 1948.

16. In a letter to Lt. Col. Alfred A. Purcell, 442nd Regimental Combat Team, July 13, 1945.

17. *Chicago Daily News,* as quoted in *Pacific Citizen,* April 29, 1944.

18. Col. Sidney F. Mashbir, "Nisei Intelligence Work in the Pacific," speech given at Twenty-Fifth Anniversary Dinner of the Military Intelligence Service, November 11, 1966, at Jack Tar Hotel, San Francisco.

19. Quoted with permission of Mrs. George Tanaka and Frederick Sawada.

20. John Tinker, *Hokubei Mainichi,* January 28, 1972.

21. *Pacific Citizen,* December 24, 1971.

22. Donald T. Hata, Jr., "The Undesirables," doctoral dissertation, University of Southern California, 1970, p. 75.

23. April 4, 1971.

24. (New York: Viking Press, 1954), p. 129.

25. Mrs. James Tanabee, speech given in *America's Largest Town Meeting of the Air,* WBBM, Chicago, February 6, 1968.

26. *The Epic of America* (Boston: Little, Brown, 1932), p. 404.

27. "The Japanese Newspapers," *Social Solidarity Among the Japanese in Seattle,* University of Washington Publications in the Social Sciences, vol. 2, no. 2 (1939), p. 119.

28. Mary Kochiyama in letter to *Hokubei Mainichi,* January 1, 1972.

29. (New York: Fleming H. Revell, 1909), p. 22.

30. Cary, p. 32.

31. (New York: Wiley, 1956), p. 57.

32. *Pacific Stars and Stripes,* August 9, 1971.

Index